BE DO SALE

Contents

SECTION FOUR:

HOW DO GURUS CREATE MORE SALES FROM THEIR CLIENTS AND CONTACTS?

FOREWORD

As every human being has a heart that is beating to keep them alive, so too does our economy have a beating heart. The beating heart of our economy is Sales. At this very moment, there are millions, if not billions, of sales transactions happening.

As you look around you, everything from the clothes you are wearing to the things on your desk, to the pictures hanging on your wall, even the quality of the oxygen you are breathing is a result of some sale being made.

Sales makes the world go around!

As salespeople, the responsibility bestowed upon us is huge as we are the curators of the trillions of dollars of commerce that is happening at any moment. As salespeople, the state of commerce is determined by how well we engage the sales relationships we have.

In the past, when someone thought of a salesperson, they thought of a guy with a big shiny grin from ear to ear in a 20 dollar suit with an overly large red tie that went past his belt buckle. Someone that was there for personal gain, with manipulative, slimy, persuasive methods and tactics trying to get you to buy something you don't even want or need.

Manipulative, persuasive tactics may have worked in the past, but today we the consumer (because we are *also* consumers) are smarter, more skeptical, and more careful because we've been taken one too many times, which causes us to pause and think hard before any sale.

This ushers in a new era of salesmanship, one that is based on looking at the buyer as a real human being with needs and wants, rather than a fish to be baited and caught.

As I read this book I felt an overwhelming sense of gratitude and awe, realizing that Erik and The GURUS Selling System answers the call of all consumers wanting to be treated with respect when engaging in a sale.

From the salesperson's perspective this book should be used as a handbook, or a guide on how to gain the trust and respect of the buyer while being compensated in the highest possible way and maintaining authenticity and honor in the sales process.

In laymen's terms it means getting paid what you are worth, without having to sell your soul by using underhanded manipulation tactics.

This book is the new way of selling, some people already do some of what Erik talks about but they don't exactly know how. This book breaks down the process on how to be authentic and genuine in every aspect of the sales process while at the same time profiting even more by using this new model of sales.

This sales masterpiece is now in your hands and don't be surprised when *The GURUS Selling System* quickly becomes the de facto standard for many *Fortune 500* companies in the months and years to come...

Treating people like they deserve to be treated...While making GOBS of cash...Brilliant!

~~ **Stephan P. Stavrakis**

CEO of *3D Thinking & Training*, Positioning Strategist and Creator of *Perceptual Positioning*

SECTION ONE

How do I become
a <u>GURUS</u> salesperson?

CHAPTER 1
BEGIN

Steve was frustrated. He had been involved in big ticket tech sales for over a dozen years. He was a "top producer." And he, like many, believed that his experience and network would keep him at his regular sales volume even though the world economy had hit the skids. He was wrong!

Despite his experience, his connections, his knowledge, his expensive suits, his witty repartee, his "never say die" attitude, his shiny Porsche and his beautiful Rolex, his sales were sinking.

His boss had called me a few weeks before and asked me if I could do some coaching with all of the sales team members to get them over their current woes. I warned Steve's boss that my methodology was not the common sales stuff. He said that "common" wasn't working, so he was ready for "uncommon."

I was having my second session with Steve and he was skeptical of the homework I was having him do. He asked me outright: "How is this GURUS stuff going to help me sell more?"

"It won't," I replied.

After a moment of odd silence Steve asked, "Then why the hell am I doing it?"

I replied…

"If you're going to do things the GURUS way, then you'll never <u>sell</u> anything ever again."

"What are you talking about?!" He asked as his face began to turn red.

I could see he was confused, angry and ready to storm out. I chose my words very carefully.

"Steve" I said "Your whole career has been spent 'selling' people. You have been very well trained in selling. And you're really good at selling."

He nodded his head in agreement.

"Now, selling," I continued, "the way you and most salespeople do it, is based on trying to convince clients to buy stuff with information, tactics and techniques. It's basically all mechanical."

Steve furrowed his brow.

I continued, "Selling used to work very well. However, now clients have more information, more choices, more things vying for their time, more reasons to hold onto their money, more pressure, and a lot less patience. To clients…

"SELL *has become a four-letter word.*"

He chuckled at that one.

"Everybody out there is using Sandler or Ziglar or SPIN or whatever. The clients are tired of being techniqued to death."

"Well, if we don't use techniques, what are we supposed to use?" Asked Steve, thoroughly confused.

"Well it's not so much about the technique. Obviously you have to DO something. The more important part is what are you BEing when you DO what you do?"

Steve responded with a blank stare. I decided to bring it closer to home.

"Do you have kids?" I asked.

"Yes," he replied.

"Do you pay attention when your kids speak to you?"

"Of course," he replied.

"Do you have friends?"

Steve rolled his eyes. "Yes!"

"Do you listen to them when they speak?"

"Of course," he said a little warily.

"Why do you listen to these people?" I asked.

"Because I care for them," he finished.

"Exactly! You respect them. You are bonded with them."

"Yes, of course," he agreed.

"And you respect what they say to you because they are being honest when they speak with you. And when they are not being up front with you, you know that too because you can sense it."

"Yes," he said.

"That is what clients want too. They have genuine wants and needs. They want to have the help of honest human beings whom they respect. They don't want to be flim-flammed with a bunch of heartless techniques to create the 'appearance' of honest communication."

Steve sat back in his chair. I could tell something had just switched over in his brain.

"So," Steve said slowly, "If I use a technique on a client but I am not BEing genuine, then it's fake, and that's 'cause I'm forcing it. But that same technique, if it comes from me BEing natural, then it has far more meaning to them."

I smiled wide.

"Yes!" I said happily. "When you give up trying to 'sell to' and instead focus on 'aligning with' the client, you will shift how you do things. And when you change how you do things, your results will change as well."

"The difference between compassionate persuasion and self-serving manipulation is all in your intent."

…I added.

"It's starting to make sense now," He said.

"It's just like Be, Do, Have if you think about it," I replied. "Most people think 'Have, Be, Do.' They look at their bank account and say 'I HAVE a million dollars in the bank, so I BE a millionaire and I can DO millionaire things' or 'I HAVE five dollars in the bank so I BE worth five dollars and I can DO five dollar things.'"

"If you follow that logic no one will ever get richer or poorer. Now obviously, that is not the case. Every day someone new becomes a millionaire and someone else stops being a millionaire."

"The deciding factor is your mind-set. When you judge yourself by what you have you will believe *that* is what you are and you will take actions based on that. You are surrendering yourself to fate and chance."

"However, when you consciously decide who you want to BE, you will DO things according to that mind-set and ultimately you will HAVE that outcome."

"So for me it's like Be, Do, Sale," said Steve.

"Precisely," I said smiling. "And what a great name for a book," I added.

"Okay," said Steve "I'm ready to BE a GURUS Salesperson."

~~~~~~~~~~~~~~

NOTE: When many people hear my opinion of "selling" they ask me why I called my process a "selling" system. This is a valid question.

The truth is that when I named *The GURUS Selling System* I was looking for a name that would instantly tell people what the system is about, in a way that was familiar to them. After all, if it was called *The GURUS Alignment System*, people would be asking me to do wheel alignments on their cars.

So, even though the name is potentially "hypocritical" it was done with the genuine intention to help people. And "genuine" is what The GURUS Selling System is all about!

☑ DO... Start with the Basics

The question I get asked most is "Where did GURUS come from?" I'd love to tell you that I planned the whole thing out. That I went and studied with many sales and marketing "gurus" and that I intended to create, not to mention name, a system based on that experience in a really cool turn of phrase (i.e. GURUS).

But the truth is that I didn't do any of that. After two and a half years of working side by side with these folks, or paying for their mentoring or attending their seminars or studying their books, CDs etc, I was able to see how they went through their sales processes.

Let me emphasize that last statement again...

I was able to SEE how they went through their sales processes!

This was the pivotal difference. All of my mentors told me what they did and how they did it. Of course, being a student of cognitive behavioral processes, I am well aware that people have habits and actions they are consciously aware of and they have many of which they are unaware.

So, my mentors were – unknowingly – holding out on me. Of course that wasn't really a problem. Since I knew they spoke / acted / thought in ways of which they were unaware, I simply modeled *everything* they did...and got all the answers I was after.

Then all I did was synthesize their processes together and it was apparent that there were five distinct phases that occurred in the sales processes of all my mentors. All I did was break them down and add in some details they had left out...or were just completely unaware of...and *The GURUS Selling System* was born.

Being an open person, I drafted a report of my discoveries that outlined the GURUS System and discussed several of the unique techniques you will discover later in this book. I then sent this report to all of the mentors I had personally studied with.

I wasn't expecting the reaction I got!

A few congratulated me on a job well done. However, many of them were unhappy. The scale went from "I don't want you telling people my secrets" to "I'm going to f***ing sue your ass!"

Although I was upset by these reactions, I was not deterred. I never have stolen – and never will steal – anyone's patented, trademarked or copyrighted material. And, more importantly, I gave names to and created processes for many tactics my mentors themselves were never aware they employed…until after I showed them.

C'est la vie!

Now, ever since I told my friends and colleagues that I was writing a book called **BE DO SALE**, the second-most-asked question I get is, "What does that mean?"

Hopefully my story about Steve explained it for you well enough. Nonetheless, if the story didn't clear it up, let me synopsize it for you.

Before you can attain *anything* you don't have, but desire, you must first BE a person who can attain that desire. By "BE" I mean that in your mind, body and soul you must BE that person. Only then can you DO the activities required to eventually HAVE what you desire.

The sad truth, however, is that most people live lives of quiet desperation. They look at what they HAVE and convince themselves that is all they can BE and they go out and DO things that recreate that reality, over and over again. It is a vicious cycle!

So, the order in which the universe allows us to create is BE…DO…HAVE.

In the realm of sales, this simply translates into BE DO SALE. That's it. That's my story and I'm sticking to it!

The GURUS Selling System simply gives structure to the BE DO SALE process, so you can actually grasp it, apply it and use it.

Of course by this point I'm sure you've been enjoying my witty stories and explanations, and I'm also sure you're chomping at the bit to learn about the GURUS System. So enough with the set up; let's dive in and examine the five phases of *The GURUS Selling System*.

I. G is for Genuine Self.

Although many salespeople hear this and think it is lip service, it is the most vital part of sales. All buyers want to trust, respect and have confidence in the salespeople they deal with, especially the salespeople they intend to do long term business with. It is impossible to have trust in, respect for or confidence in someone you are unsure about.

By being genuine you take that element of doubt off the table. Yes, someone may not like the genuine you, and if that happens that is great. It is better to know up front who you will and will not get along with. This gives you a lot more free time to find clients you can genuinely connect with.

Like I always say, "I'd rather be sure of my enemies than doubt my friends."

II. U is for Unique Sales Persona.

A Unique Sales Persona is how you bring the most enjoyable, memorable and intriguing aspects of yourself out in sales.

Every salesperson wants to differentiate themselves from the pack. Yet most of them act, think, dress, walk and talk like everybody else. This assures that they will blend in, which assures they will be forgotten. As a GURUS Salesperson you stand out without being thrown out, which makes you memorable without a doubt.

III. R is for Rapport Building.

Rapport is how GURUS salespeople connect with and begin to align with clients.

Without rapport there will never be any sale or, if there is a sale, it will be a one-shot deal born from the buyer's necessity and lack of options. In that situation there is no loyalty and you will have to create more and more leads to make up for the lack of recurring business.

IV. The second U is for UBP or Unique Buying Position.

The UBP is the point where the buyer's deepest pain connects with their deepest problem. This is the point you want to get to with every client.

Although this may sound commonplace or even easy, it is anything but. The inability of most salespeople to find and effectively work with the buyer's UBP is the reason most sales never happen. Without question, it is the most important point in any sales situation.

V. S is for Sales Ally.

This is the point of the process where you get to enjoy your newfound connection, and well-deserved business, with the client. And, being a devoted GURUS Salesperson, you also commit to staying bonded to and connected with the client at all times. This is what other trainers aspire to when they throw around the term "trusted advisor." However, in this case, you have leverage as well as trust.

Ultimately, the GURUS process is designed to help you get to a higher level of thinking or, as we say, to take the high road.

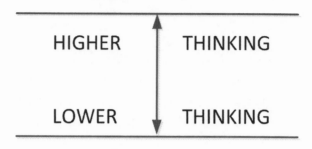

Client-Centered
Aligned with client
"I want to serve you"

HIGHER **THINKING**

LOWER **THINKING**

Self-Centered
No alignment with client
"I want to sell you"

When you're thinking at a higher level your thoughts are free of the self-centered junk that random emotions or concerns bring up. You will focus on the client. You will communicate more easily and more meaningfully with clients. And, of course, you will make more sales more easily, which is the whole point, isn't it?

☑ THE PRESUPPOSITIONS

Many systems will teach you commandments or rules and tell you that you have to operate by them or else. As a GURUS Salesperson you will learn that you can, should and will question everything you do at one time or another.

That being said, it is useful to have some fundamental framework so that you have an idea what you're doing and where you're going. After all, if you're going to change and improve any game, you first have to know the way the game is currently played.

Therefore, I have compiled eleven presuppositions. I call them presuppositions because they are exactly that: Things you "suppose" are true before engaging a client.

You may follow them as is, adjust them as needed, scrap them altogether or add to them if you desire. By the way, if you do add to them or change any of them, please let me know what you added and why; I am always up for learning more.

I. The client's needs supersede your own

In a world where salespeople are hell-bent on "making their numbers" it is very easy to put your own needs before the client's. When you do that, however, you automatically come into the sales situation with an agenda. This cuts off the possibility of purely open and honest communication between you and the client, which flies in the face of what GURUS is all about.

When you can put aside your own desires and focus on the needs of the client without distraction you will be there to solve their problems. This unfettered view allows you to align with the client completely, so that when you recommend solutions you can speak honestly and have your words taken that way. This makes your word your bond.

That kind of integrity is worth more than a million testimonials!

II. If it doesn't flow let it go

Far too often when a salesperson gets what they believe is the faintest hint of interest from a prospect they will keep going after that person and the would-be sale doggedly. When they become fixated like this they lose the awareness that would tell them the sale isn't going to happen or, if it is, it's going to be a long hard battle with a diminished ROI that ultimately isn't worth it.

As a GURUS Salesperson you know that how the situation *feels* is far more important than what someone says. You know you only want to deal with clients that are thrilled to work with you and situations that are enjoyable, move forward naturally and easily and leave no doubt that the sale will ultimately be yours.

III. Solution first, sale second

Many times when a salesperson is working with a client on a problem, they can get to a point where they agree on a problem being a "problem." At this point the salesperson, even with the best of intentions, can blurt out a solution to the problem and try to close the sale, just to lose the deal because the solution was too shallow or off base.

As a GURUS salesperson you realize that getting to the client's problem is only one part of the process. You must also create and agree upon a solution with the client. Once you and the client have co-created a true full-scope solution, the sale is yours by default.

IV. You are equals always

Some salespeople, even hooty-snooty ones, have a tendency to put their clients on pedestals. This can be because they truly believe that the clients deserve to be idealized or because they are desperate for a sale and are basically groveling at their client's feet. Whatever the reason...

This always ends badly.

When the client perceives that they are "above" you they never respect you fully. Ultimately that lack of respect leads to a lack of loyalty, and a more self-assured salesperson steals them away.

Conversely, some salespeople look down on their clients. They see them as numbers on the monthly quota or just simply don't like them. When clients perceives that they are "under" the salesperson they are dealing with they will automatically feel disrespected and look for another vendor that treats them like a person.

As a GURUS Salesperson you know that every man, woman

and child on this earth is your equal. Therefore, you always treat everyone, including clients, with the humble self-assuredness that is the bearing of all great leaders, like a Dalai Lama, a Jesus or a JFK.

V. The client's problem is not a "problem"

Many salespeople are able to truly bond with their clients. They have true heart and are able to really see the world through the client's eyes. This is great for rapport but lousy for sales.

When a salesperson becomes truly sympathetic with the issues the client is facing, they can begin to view the world through the limiting beliefs of the client. At that point, when the client says why they can't solve the problem, the salesperson agrees because they are blinded by the client's reality. In other words, they have bought the client's self-limiting beliefs.

As a GURUS Salesperson you create rapport with your clients easily and honestly. You even get to the point of sympathy, but only long enough to see the client's limited thinking. Then you shift into objective empathy, which allows you to be aligned with the client without being blinded by their limited view.

VI. Alignment trumps all

Many salespeople go into a sales situation with an agenda, like a series of steps they want to "get" the clients into or questions they want to ask or things they want to hear the client say. Basically, they are trying to force a client through a process.

Though this type of approach is useful for tracking and measuring it is not very good for truly connecting with clients or helping them with their needs.

As a GURUS Salesperson you realize that true rapport, understanding, respect and confidence flow from one source: Alignment.

Alignment is just that…being totally aligned with your client in all aspects…thoughts, feelings and actions.

True alignment also makes you more attractive to do business with.

Alignment facilitates trust in you and bypasses the buyer's need for a "reason" to do business with you.

They are simply compelled to do business with you from inside themselves.

VII. The client's pain and the problem are not the same

Few salespeople are skilled at getting to the deeper level of pains or problems with clients. Those that can build effective rapport and get to deeper levels with clients are often unable to separate the client and the problem.

The client's problem is a tangible logistical issue that can ultimately be resolved with the application of tangible resources (products and/or services). However…

The client's "pain" is their own internal perception.

Example: A client's Problem may be that they are unable to hire the right employees for their company, resulting in high turnover, lowered productivity, more time disciplining and managing staff, etc. But their Pain is the fear of losing their job if they don't make better choices in hiring.

As a GURUS Salesperson you know that Pain and Problem are separate and equal. With this understanding you are better able to communicate with clients, by helping them to separate the pain and problem in their own mind, which allows them to focus more logically on a solution to the problem while lessening the emotional burden of their pain.

VIII. Your "communication" is measured by the response that you get

Many salespeople go into a sales situation armed with a script or set of information they are determined to tell the client no matter what. They believe, mistakenly, that "the script always works" or "the client can't say 'no' once they hear this…"

This focus on 'I have to say my piece' versus 'Is the client understanding and agreeing with what I am telling them?' causes an instant break in rapport and alignment and will ultimately lose you the sale.

As a GURUS Salesperson you pay attention to your words and you also pay very close attention to the effect those words have on your client. You know that just because you say something to a client, it doesn't mean they heard it the way you meant it. This awareness allows you to detect and eliminate any misunderstandings and confusion when they happen, so the whole process flows faster and easier.

IX. There is no failure, only feedback

Every salesperson has things they hope for. It could be more leads per day, more face to face meetings, more closed deals, more referrals, etc. To achieve these outcomes they will take certain actions based on outcomes they believe will be theirs. But when the outcome is not what they desired, they deem it a failure.

Example: In order to close more deals, a salesperson may try a new technique they just learned. They believe the technique will create a more immediate need in the client and seal the deal faster. But after trying it on ten clients and losing all the deals, they call the technique a "failure." Or, worse yet, they call themselves a "failure."

As a GURUS salesperson you know that failure can only exist if you give up completely. You know that…

As long as you keep working
at something, there is no "failure!"

This being the case, you see the difference between the results you desired and the results you get in any endeavor as feedback. You are then able to use that feedback as the basis for analysis and correction. This makes each successive attempt merely a test. And you know that testing and adjusting according to feedback will ultimately produce the results you desire.

X. The most flexible person will control the sales process

Many salespeople go into sales situations trying to be in control of the process. They have hard and fast steps, scripts, phases, presentations, schedules, prices, etc. They believe these tools and procedures will allow them to dictate the flow of the sales process.

When someone doesn't fit into the "box" they have created, that client is automatically a "bad client" or "lost cause."

As a GURUS salesperson you know that no two clients, schedules, problems or sales processes are ever alike. Therefore, you never look to control the process. You merely look to remain in control of yourself and to adapt to whatever situation arises.

In this way you are just as ingenious when the going is rough as when it is easy. This flexible ingenuity allows you to always see the situation objectively and to overcome any roadblock that might pop up between you and the finished deal.

XI. Resistance in a client is a sign of lack of alignment

In virtually every sales situation salespeople get resistance from clients. The resistance can be as minor as not liking a meeting location, all the way up to screaming irrationally about a change in pricing. There is no telling when resistance will appear.

When met with resistance most salespeople will usually drop into accommodation mode for minor resistance, justification mode for moderate resistance or defensive mode for severe resistance. Each of these modes is based on "dealing" with the client and their perceived issues.

As a GURUS salesperson you know that...

Resistance is not a situation to be "dealt" with!

Instead it is a misalignment between what you understand about a situation and what the client understands.

With this understanding you are able to put aside the momentary "issue," drop back into rapport building and alignment generation and repair the misalignment between you and the client, which strengthens their respect for, and trust in, you.

Chapter 2
BE Aware

It would be remiss of me to say that being a GURUS salesperson is easy. If that were true then everyone would be a GURUS salesperson. Like the path that all great leaders take, it has challenges, but the challenges are worth it and the reward is the living of a legendary life and the creation of legendary sales.

Nonetheless, there are some challenges you should be aware of, so…

☑ THE CHALLENGES

I. Challenge – Living in truth

From birth we are conditioned to act and behave in certain ways. It is trained into us that if we don't do what the "big people" want us to do, we could get smacked or sent to bed hungry.

As we mature we gain some insight into our childhood conditioning, which gives us some freedom. This allows us to let go of some ways that don't serve us. However, the fear of "big people" and their reactions rears its ugly head in high end sales.

> *The people with big hands have now been replaced by people with big budgets.*

Instinctively we want to please these new "big people." Very quickly we dress like them, speak like them, approach them humbly, try not to bother them, etc. We basically turn them into a new version of our parents.

As a GURUS salesperson you always live in the truth of who you are. That means being who you are…who you *really* are.

This means that you say what you feel. You present yourself as you feel best. You decide who you want to be, regardless of what other people think, and then you bring that person to the party.

This can be difficult because the first fear for salespeople when they hear this is "what if I lose a sale because the client doesn't like my shirt, or what I say, or how I act?"

It is true that you may not align with certain clients naturally. And that is good! You will instantly know who you have a good chance of aligning with and who is a waste of time. After all, even if a buyer has deep pockets, if you have to sell out and pretend to be something you're not to get the deal, you have already lost something far more precious: Yourself.

II. **Challenge – Bypassing comfort zones**

The truth is that people need patterns to live. If things like how to tie your shoelaces changed everyday you'd never get out of nursery school. Heck, you might not even make it to nursery school!

Humans instinctively look for set ways of doing things day in and day out. This allows us to know where we are going and where we have been. These "comfort zones" of how to do what we do serve a valuable purpose. They can also be the very things that keep us from getting what we want.

Every salesperson has comfort zones within their sales process: Whom they call, when they call, how they dress, how much they ask for, where they look for leads, how they try to close deals, etc. Virtually every step of their sales work process is based on comfort zones.

Of course, if what you were doing to create sales was giving you the results you desire, you probably wouldn't be reading this book right now! So at least one, and probably many, of…

> ### *The comfort zones within your current sales process are what hold you back.*

As a GURUS salesperson you will feel and appreciate your comfort zones and also bypass them as needed.

This means that you will become more in-tune with yourself and gain awareness of when you "hit the wall" of limitation. And, you will also move past it once you are aware of it.

The concept of having "no limitations" is both awe-inspiring and scary. As human beings we are trained to think we are "just like everyone." The truth is that you are equally as valuable as every other being on this planet and, simultaneously, you are also unique.

Therefore, to use any other human being as the measuring stick for your potential is foolish. Even the greatest salesperson of all time is no match for you once you choose to be truly limitless.

Also, remember that your buyers have their own comfort zones. By being the living embodiment of "no limitations" you will automatically inspire respect and even awe from them. This is a powerful position to come from in any sales situation.

III. Challenge – Letting go of steps or scripts and trusting yourself

One of the great appeals of many sales systems available out there is their "plug and play" approach. You simply take their exact steps, scripts and techniques and "plug" in your product or service.

The obvious benefit to these systems is in their ease of use. You don't have to think, and if you follow their steps exactly, you'll get a certain amount of conversions virtually guaranteed.

There is a certain amount of comfort, if not security, in putting faith into these "connect the dots" systems.

The downside is that clients soon grow tired of the by-rote process and look for more interesting salespeople to work with. In response, the lead generation portion of the system becomes used more often than any other part and eventually the market is saturated by, and disgusted with, the system.

Even though the client may not know the system that is being used, they can sense they have "heard this before," and...

The sale is DOA at this point!

By being a GURUS salesperson you move beyond set patterns and binding scripts. You allow what happens to happen and you respond naturally. You trust in yourself. You trust that someone – call it God, Allah, Buddha, the Universe, the Great Spirit – is looking out for you, and all will work out as it should.

Like walking down a hallway while looking at your Blackberry, you just "know" the floor will be there to meet your feet. You don't need to check before each step.

Of course, trusting yourself that much can be a challenge for almost anyone.

IV. Challenge – Letting go of expectations

This may be the most difficult challenge. It is probably the one I myself struggle with most and that is because it's automatic.

Whenever we engage in any activity we do so because we fast-forward in our minds and see an outcome. We are expecting the outcome we dreamed of. And yet, we never get exactly what we expected.

If we are a little off course, like expecting the cake we're baking to rise to four inches but having it only rise to three, then we aren't really thrown. But when we are way off course, like expecting to close a deal we've been working on for six months just to be told they gave the sale to another company, we can be sent spiraling.

The "effort" you perceive in doing sales is directly proportionate to the amount of expectation you attach to each activity. If you have a lot of expectations, you have a lot of effort. No expectation, no effort.

GURUS salespeople, being genuine people who want to help first and foremost and are focused on the client and trust in themselves, have no expectations. As such you are able to handle any outcome, be it sale or no sale, with peaceful equilibrium.

I know the very idea of letting go of expectations in sales sounds heretical. Yet, if you want to be able to embrace your true potential, it is vital.

The truth is that even the loftiest of expectations is still a limitation. That limitation or boundary can make you feel like a failure if you don't reach it, and it can stop you from reaching untold wonders if you do reach and stop.

Also, expectations stop the natural "flow" of things. When things "aren't going our way" and we fear not reaching our expectations, we will tend to try a forced course correction. This kind of activity breaks rapport with our client and the flow of what is happening and will ultimately cost us a friend and a sale.

V.   Challenge – Really changing

As I have alluded to in the other challenges listed so far, no one likes change. Therefore, change itself is a challenge.

People are used to being who they are, what they are and how they are. Whether or not they like or enjoy *who*, *what* or *how* they are currently being doesn't matter. Simply being that way is what they know. It is "reality."

As I always tell my clients…

> ## *"You can't prepare for change.*
> ## *You can only commit to it."*

As you are now changing into a GURUS Salesperson you will feel out of sorts at times. This is a good thing! As you embrace the GURUS framework and work through the challenges you will know you are making progress, first by feeling weird and then, second, by feeling that the "weird" is now you.

Changing your essential self may sound like an almost ridiculous length to go just to generate more sales, and if this were about just upping your conversion ratio a few points I would agree with you. Of course, you don't need this system to help with a few measly points' increase. Just work a little harder and you'll get a little more.

But if you are looking to CHANGE on a global scale how you work and you want sales increases in factors of tens or more, then change is not only necessary…it is inevitable.

Honestly, the only way to improve your sales is to improve yourself.

So, enjoy it!

VI. Challenge – Dealing with the bigness of high end sales

True high end sales are like no other sales on the planet. The numbers are bigger. The egos are bigger. The titles are bigger. The stakes are bigger. No matter what part we discuss, it's bigger.

In this environment it is easy for neophytes to lose confidence and go looking for cover. Even the occasional seasoned pro can lose their cool and drop the ball. It can overwhelm you before you know it. And it is all based on the perceived size of the sale.

Of course, as a GURUS salesperson, you realize that size doesn't matter and everything is relative. To a three-billion-dollar company a five-million-dollar purchase is a drop in the bucket, even though it may be twenty times your annual salary.

This is also true of intangibles such as titles and experience. The veteran CEO of a *Fortune 50* company may hold an image of himself as stern and aloof, and he might expect instant admiration because of that.

Yet you realize that he goes to the bathroom just like you do, and that he has base needs and desires like everyone else. This allows you to see that there really is no bigness or smallness, only sameness.

VII. Challenge – Putting in time for money

"You have to put in the time." This old ditty is drilled into the head of virtually every employee, and follows us through our lives as we move up the corporate food chain. It is the basis for employers wanting eight to ten hours a day of "work" from their employees.

It is the protestant work ethic and it never dies.

Of course, as many studies prove, most folks don't "work" the whole eight to ten hours. The average employee really only puts in about two hours of work a day and, personally, I think it's even less than that.

This antiquated model makes salespeople focus their attention far too much on time and tasks rather than leverage and results.

GURUS salespeople realize that they are business owners and entrepreneurs, even if someone else signs their paychecks. This shift from 'employee' to 'owner' allows them a perspective that is far more powerful and far-reaching than even their bosses have.

To a GURUS salesperson, sales is no longer a task to be done but a project to be optimized. This opens the door for creativity and limitless leverage.

When time is the yardstick there is never enough. When results are the yardstick anything is possible.

VIII. Challenge – Things being too easy

As you deal with change more easily, bypass comfort zones, trust in yourself and let go of scripts, and begin to leverage far more profits from far less activity, it can almost seem as if things become "too easy."

This can be a very trying time for folks as they fully transition over to the GURUS way.

We've all heard tales of lottery winners who won millions of dollars just to end up bankrupt and homeless five years later. This happens when people get something they haven't prepared for. When you achieve sales success freedom, it can also happen.

However, now that you are on the path of the GURUS, you understand that sales was never meant to be hard, and success in business should be easy when you are doing the right things for the right reasons.

CHAPTER 3
<u>BE</u> GENUINE

"How many cares one loses when one decides not to be something but to be someone." - Coco Chanel

Clients often tell me that they don't "feel genuine" in many of their sales situations. They then ask me how to "be more genuine."

The funny thing is that their first statement is the answer to their question. Being genuine is all in how you *feel*. You can tell when you are out of alignment with your true self even a little.

Yes, there's that word again: Alignment. You see, before you can ever hope to be in full alignment with a client you first have to be in full alignment with yourself. And the easiest way to know is to gauge how you feel.

Now, I agree with you, falling out of alignment can happen pretty easily and completely without malice. The reason most salespeople fall out of alignment is the same reason any structure falls out of alignment... attempting to compensate.

Imagine a well balanced tree, big, tall and strong. Now take a small passenger car and plop it into the branches on one side of the tree. Instantly the tree bends to compensate for this new weight that has been added. Take away the car, and the tree goes back to normal. This is called Structural Integrity.

Now, let's take a salesperson who goes into a sales job open, honest and genuine. Soon after they get their job they get the "weight" of a quota (usually unrealistic) dumped on them. Then they get the "weight" of paperwork dumped on them. Then they go to client meetings and the get the "weight" of client expectations dumped on them. Then they see the potential for a sale that is just out of reach and so they reach out for that "weight" too. These are just a few examples.

Imagine what the tree would look like now!

So, the secret of getting back into alignment, to your genuine self is to dump the "weights." You must feel as comfortable as possible with every element of your sales job and process.

When you feel comfortable about yourself you are being genuine.

☑ DO... Choose Right from the Start

One major way that salespeople set themselves up to be misaligned or fake right from the start is to choose what they are going to sell based on money. Simply, if you don't have a genuine love or respect for what you sell, and you don't believe that it is the BEST product or service available for the problem it solves, then you shouldn't be selling it.

I have spoken to thousands of salespeople who pride themselves on having sold items in a dozen different industries. And when I ask them why they left their first, second, third, etc. job they say, "Better pay."

I then ask if they would recommend any of the previous items they sold even if they didn't get a cent for it. They always say "no" or ask, "Why should I?"

This is Fake 101!

A GURUS salesperson goes about their job choice differently. They will find a product or service they believe in or a field of business they enjoy. Then they will seek to work with the company they like most or at least a company whose goods they can genuinely respect and feel good about.

Almost every salesperson who has long term trouble with their sales has that trouble because they are not genuinely connected with what they sell. If your loyalty is to the money you make from your job, you radiate that energy to your clients. So don't be surprised when they are only loyal to you until someone cheaper comes along. You have created a loyalty that is only price deep.

☑ DO... Mind Your Emotions

Now, even when you are being totally genuine it doesn't guarantee you're bringing your "A-Game" with you. You can be the most genuine person in the world, but if you're in a crappy mental or emotional state you'll have crappy sales. Remember...

Feel good, sell good. Feel bad, sell bad.

Basically, your sales performance is truly state-dependent. In other words, whatever state of mind you are in will have far more impact on how well or how poorly you sell than the words you say or the presentation you make/give.

And when you venture into the high pressure, cutthroat world of high end sales it can be a true strain on even the most Zen of us. So, it is vitally important that you handle your internal sales process before starting to tackle your external one.

Let's take a look at how to control your mind, emotions and feelings.

☑ DO... Keep This in Mind for the Rest of Your Sales Life

One of the main reasons salespeople have a difficult time keeping their minds and emotions in check is because they are unfairly vilified on a regular basis. There are tons of studies that show that the average person has an unfavorable opinion of "salespeople."

This is utter crap as far as I am concerned! Just like cops, firefighters and teachers, salespeople are vitally necessary and forever misjudged and overlooked....until there is a need.

Salespeople are superheroes!

They should be honored and respected. They put themselves out there day after day to move the products and services that keep this world running...literally!

Take any person who has a bad opinion of salespeople and ask them what they do for a living. They'll puff out their chest and say something like, "I'm an accountant for ABC Corp." Then ask them what ABC Corp does. They'll tell you that ABC Corp. sells widgets. Then ask them who sells the widgets that ABC makes. They'll say the salespeople. Now ask them how they'd get paid if the salespeople did not sell the widgets that ABC made. Case closed!

Salespeople are vital! Including you!

The only reason salespeople have the reputation they do is because there are some bad apples. And although this same amount of rotten apples can be found in any occupation, because salespeople have a higher profile than most, they get more flack.

The rotten apples...salespeople who use their skills to manipulate others... tarnish all of us.

However, there is hope, even for the rotten apples. Within this book you shall find it. It may not be salvation per se, but so long as it helps you to be a "person" within the salesperson you are, it is enough.

☑ DO... Control Your Emotions Instantly with Your Body

Everybody likes to get what they want faster. Yet most salespeople will try to "just deal" with their emotional state until they get some free time so they can work on it then...usually with a beer.

GURUS Salespeople know that there is a much faster way to get back to a better state of mind and better sales almost instantly. Use your body.

The results we see in our lives come from this simple process: Thoughts plus emotions lead to feelings. Feelings lead to actions. Actions lead to results.

When your thoughts and emotions are crappy, you will have crappy feelings. When you feel crappy you will do crappy things. When you do crappy things you will get crappy results. And vice versa.

The secret to short circuiting this process is called PDA or Posture Determines Attitude.

The Action part of the process is performed by your body, whether that be making a phone call, writing a letter, doing a presentation, etc. it's all done via your physical body. When your mind and emotions are negative, ultimately your body is negative too. Your shoulders will droop. You will speak low or not at all. Your energy level will be down.

Now, imagine being in that negative state and then simply standing up straight, taking a deep breath. Laughing out loud for no reason. Maybe you could even jump around and scream "I'm a chicken" (as long as you're alone). It sounds ridiculous, right? Good. Get up and do it right now!

I dare you!

Hopefully, you did it and you felt silly. Maybe you didn't do it because you thought you'd feel silly. Either way you're right. And…

Silly beats the crap out of crappy any day.

But let's say you're with clients and can't jump around. You can easily stand up straight, breathe deeply and put a smile on your face. The funny thing is that the forced smile will become a real one before you know it.

The whole reason this process works – every time – is because your thoughts, emotions, feelings and actions need to be in alignment in order for you to work.

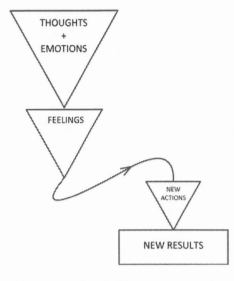

It's impossible to piss and moan when you feel happy. It's impossible to feel miserable and laugh happily. When you shift your actions, your feelings, emotions and thoughts will shift in order to create internal alignment again as quickly as possible.

Normally, people just allow their thoughts and emotions to control their feelings and their feelings to control their body. They do this unconsciously. Now you are going to consciously control your body's posture and actions. Once you change what the body is doing then the feelings look to the heart and brain to plug in new emotions and thoughts that reinforce what the body is doing…like feeling silly!

☑ DO… Talk to a Higher Power

Being a high end salesperson can make you feel alone if not lonely. You are "alone" because the sale usually rests on your shoulders. Win or lose it's all up to you. That kind of pressure can create a lot of negative thoughts in your head.

Most salespeople will just "suck it up" and "take it like a man" (even some women!). Though this might make them believe that they are tough, it also lends itself to stress, burnout and breakdowns.

However, as one of my GURUS mentors taught me early on, "You are never alone."

Imagine if you could take all your negative self-talk, your fears about not making quota, losing your job, looking foolish in front of clients and all that other garbage in your head and just give it away. Well, you can! Just give it to your higher power!

Now I am not a religious man, so I will not be telling you which god to pray to or even to pray to a god for that matter. Of course, if you are a religious person, then your deity of choice will work just fine too.

Personally, I call my "higher power" **Source** or **The Great Spirit**. However, again…

This isn't about ideology. It's about functionality.

This is how my Mentor explained it to me. "When we carry a burden alone in our minds we create a closed loop. Like a rat in a cage, the negative thoughts have nowhere to go. This is why they can spiral out of control. When you have some kind of higher power you can surrender all your fears, doubts, worries and concerns to it and voila, they are gone. Remember, the key word is 'surrender,' not 'share.' If you 'share' something it can possibly come back to you."

The cynics out there will say, "But that doesn't really get rid of all your fears. In reality they are still there."

There is <u>no</u> fear in "reality!!"

If Fear does exist I dare you to show me a photograph of it!

Fears and worries are constructs of the mind. We lump together a group of situations we are currently involved with, project them into the future, imagine outcomes we don't like, and then we get frightened! Voila! We have created fears and worries!

Since fear and doubt only exist in the mind they can only **cease** to exist by removing them from the mind. That is why "surrendering" them to your higher power works. You create a doorway through which they can leave. And you give them to someone or something that is far more powerful than they (or you) are.

This works with one condition: You must have full faith in your higher power. If you do not believe in a higher power…be it God, Allah, the Universe, the Great Spirit, Buddha, etc. (or even a doughnut)… then this doesn't work.

Of course, if you believe in your fears, you also have to believe there is something that can get rid of them. After all, everything - <u>everything</u> - has an opposite. That's not just me talking. That's physics. Look it up!

☑ DO... Get a Handle on It

It's very easy to go from relaxed to overwhelmed in a matter of moments in the world of high end sales. This is the time that most salespeople wish they could just "get a handle on things."

GURUS salespeople know they can always "get a handle" on any runaway emotion. And though virtually all of my mentors had ways of doing this, one of them had a technique I personally use and love. She called it "The HIT" (Handle It Technique).

How-To: Do a HIT

1. Imagine a handle attached to some sort of slide or pivot point. I personally use an image of those old fashioned throttle controls they used to use on the bridges of large ships, but you can use anything you want. It just has to have a handle and a series of numbers from 1 to 10 on it.

2. Name the emotion you are feeling: Fear, Doubt, Sadness, etc. Now, see it written below the handle.

3. Gauge how strongly you feel that emotion on a scale from 1 to 10. And whatever number comes to you naturally, see the handle start over that number.

4. SEE – in your imagination - your hand reach out and grab the handle. And see an unpleasantly colored glow emanating from the handle mechanism. Maybe gooey green or blood red.

5. FEEL the handle in your hand. For me, I feel the worn wood of the handle.

6. HEAR an unpleasant sound coming from the handle mechanism. You can imagine something like the buzz of insects or an irritating shriek.

7. Push the handle down toward 1. There should be some resistance, like you are actually pushing the handle of a lever.

As you push the handle further down see the glow begin to fade. Hear the sound begin to die down. Keep pushing until you reach 1 when the glow disappears and the sound is no more.

You will find that the negative emotion is now gone.

Of course nature abhors a vacuum, so if you don't decide what to fill that emotional space with, nature will. And…

Nature might fill it with something you don't like.

Therefore, you can also do this entire process in reverse to create a positive emotion.

Simply see the name of the emotion you want to create written below the handle. Start from number 1 and push the handle upward. This time see a powerful glow growing and hear energizing music getting louder. Keep going until you crescendo and boom! You are "handling" your emotions like a pro.

☑ DO... Go Over Your Client's Head

When sitting face to face with a potential client it can sometimes be difficult to tell if they really like you and are interested in what you're talking about or if they are just politely nodding and watching the clock.

If you have ever watched sporting events where the participants are judged, like gymnastics or diving, you'll see that the judges assign a score to what they have just watched. In a similar way…

Clients are scoring their connection with you.

The nervousness that comes upon salespeople in these situations is based upon guessing at their "score." They imagine that because the client isn't doing what they expect the connection isn't there or it is faltering. This leads to the salesperson trying harder to connect. But trying harder can often backfire because it usually makes the client think that you're desperate.

So, what are you to do?

Well, if you're a GURUS salesperson, you go over their head!

Simply imagine the score you think the client has of you hovering over their head, like a 2 or a 5. Then steadily tick it up until you reach 10.

Now this might sound a little "out there." But trust me, it works.

Why does it work? Because we act in accordance with how we perceive ourselves. In other words, however we *think* we're doing is how we act. If we imagine we are making a 3 connection with a client, we will get nervous, lose our higher level communication skills, and blabber ourselves out of the sale. So, we create the 3 we feared.

Conversely, if we imagine we are making a 10 connection – real or not – we will relax, access better communication skills and improve the connection. This is akin to when athletes "see only the goal." They eliminate the obstacles from their minds. When you turn a low number into a 10 you have eliminated the imaginary obstacle of the poor connection.

Once you see yourself as a 10, you will walk, talk, think and act like the 10 you desire to be.

☑ DO... Show Them You're the King

By its very nature high end sales denotes big money. So, big numbers are par for the course. Nonetheless, there are times when there is just a HUGE amount of money on the line with a potential deal.

In these situations every meeting or phone call with a client can be pivotal. This kind of pressure can lead to a salesperson feeling inadequate or like they want to "bring more to the game."

They may look to their idols for inspiration, perhaps secretly wishing their idols could go in and do the meeting for them. Of course, when you are a GURUS salesperson, you know that your idol can go into the meeting for you!

Imagine if your idol is someone like Zig Ziglar. You wish you could simply trade places with him, so you could have his experience, confidence, presence and creativity in the meeting. It would be like bringing King Arthur and Excalibur to a knife fight.

You'd simply dominate the room with your power.

Well, it is basically that easy.

How-To: Be the King (or Queen)

1. Choose who you'd like to be. Make sure that this person is the best choice for the situation. Clint Eastwood is tough, but he may not be the right personality for a meeting to discuss software requirements.

2. See the person standing before you about 2 or 3 feet away, with their back to you.

3. See them doing what they do best, like Zig engaging a huge audience with one of his stories. See the crowd. Hear the crowd. Feel the temperature of the auditorium or stadium. See details, like doorways on the back wall. Hear someone clearing their throat. Feel the energy in the room. BE there!

4. See the person glow brighter and brighter until they are almost too bright to look at.

5. See the person become transparent. You can see the crowd right through them.

6. Feel any negative energy in your body drop down to your feet. Shake yourself to make sure it all falls down.

7. Pull one of your feet out of the negative energy pile and step into your idol. Then pull the other foot out and step into the person entirely.

8. Feel all their power in you. See what they see. Hear what they hear. Breathe with their lungs. Speak with their voice. Move with their body. You are them. They are you.

Now, go into your meeting!

You will find that as you BE your idol you will actually BE more yourself. This is because your idol simply activates aspects of yourself that you normally leave behind when going into sales meetings. And the only reason you really wanted the idol to help you was so they could bring those aspects of YOU out when needed.

When you're done, simply step forward out of your idol. Now turn around and see them standing there facing you, still glowing.

See a circle of light appear at their feet and see them disappear down into it. As they fade down into the circle, the circle shrinks and the center hollows out. When they are gone you are left with a glowing crown.

Reach down and pick up the crown, then place it on your head. You are now the king...or queen, as the case may be.

Their energy is now with you always. And if you ever need a real pick-me-up, simply take the crown off your head and drop it on the floor and go through the process again.

Now, at this point you might think…

"This is all really silly."

And I agree with you!

Of course, letting random thoughts and self-created stress control how you feel or act is also really silly, isn't it?

So, if you're going to be "silly" anyway, you might as well make it a silliness that works *for* you instead of *against* you. Just don't expect people to call you "Your majesty', because *that* really would be silly!

CHAPTER 4
<u>BE</u> UNMOTIVATED

"Self-actualization equals sales-actualization!" - Erik Luhrs

Of the sales managers who contact me I'd have to say 90% – 95% always ask the same question: "How can I motivate my salespeople?" The same holds true for most of the salespeople who contact me. They too want to know how to stay motivated.

The truth is:
You can't motivate or stay motivated!

Now, I know there are books, seminars, and programs devoted to teaching exactly how to do just this. And although pretty much all of them have techniques in them that will tell you how to get some more activity out of yourself, ultimately they fall short.

You see, motivation is fleeting. It is merely an emotional state that comes upon us and makes us do a different activity than we were doing until that new activity is done.

Example: Yard work. The thought of cutting the grass is one that most homeowners like to avoid, because it isn't much fun. And it is only when the lawn starts to get ugly enough that a person feels motivated enough to stop couch-surfing and start mowing. Once the lawn is cut, back to the couch we go.

Now, if "motivation," as it is portrayed in the self-help media, actually worked then the couch-surfer would be out there cutting the lawn every day, not waiting until looking at the lawn actually hurt.

GURUS salespeople don't worry about motivation. They focus on <u>inspiration</u> instead.

Inspiration is actually the overall strategy. Motivation is simply a temporary tactic within that strategy.

When you are inspired you will create motivation again and again to keep doing the necessary activities to create what you are inspired to create.

Let's use the lawn again. Let's imagine a homemaker who loves plants and flowers. She is inspired to landscape her property. So she gets motivated to sketch out the property and how she wants it. Then she gets motivated to go to Home Depot to get the necessary tools and equipment (with little regard for cost, I might add). Then she gets motivated to turn the soil. Then she gets motivated to build small retaining walls… You get the picture.

Ultimately, she gets the landscaped property she wants, and since it has to be maintained regularly, she has created a situation that keeps her inspired and constantly calls upon her to get motivated to do things.

So, the question to ask of yourself or your team is…

"How do I get *inspired* to create more sales?"

Inspiration is a state of BEing. Like being in your body. You have two arms and legs and that is just what is (no offense to my amputee readers).

When you BE inspired you don't need tricks or techniques to make you do what has to be done to follow your inspiration. You do it happily.

Of course, it is obvious form the state of our world that most humans, let alone salespeople, are not inspired. It isn't that there is nothing to inspire them in the world. In fact there are more than enough options in the world to help some be inspired every moment for the rest of their lives.

The dilemma is that inspiration is a choice. And most people choose to be hired and fired rather than inspired. They choose to let other people be inspired leaders, after whom they can follow and serve. Although this is normal, it is also unhealthy.

GURUS Salespeople choose inspiration.

Now, if you know what truly inspires you to your core then you are ahead of the curve. If you don't have something that inspires you, then…..

☑ DO... Find Inspiration

Since most people aren't consciously inspired by something, a valid question would be, "how do I find something to inspire me?"

What you actually want to find is an inspiration that lends itself to action. For the purpose of high end sales you will be looking for an inspiration that will create within you the self-motivation to do your sales activities over and over again.

Inspiration actually means to be "in spirit." Therefore whatever you choose to be inspired by must be something that touches your spirit.

This is why money doesn't work.

It is a material thing and cannot transcend to spirit. Likewise, promotions, extra time off and other perks also fail to be inspirational.

So what inspires you? Let's find out. Ask yourself some questions like these...

- What do you love or respect about the items you sell?

- How do you know that what you sell is the best choice available to solve the problem(s) it solves?

- What change(s), regardless of size, do you wish to make in the world that will benefit others? And how does what you sell help that?

- What ideals does your company espouse, publicly or privately, that let you know they want the same change you do?

- Aside from your sales work, how else do you pursue this change in your life?

- When you dream about the future, after your time on earth is done, what is different because you lived?

- Do you dare to dream? If not, what would you dream if you could?

- What is the status quo (or "given") in your business or the world you wish you didn't have to accept?

As you can see, these questions are truly questions about your legacy. If you want to create legendary sales you must be a legendary BEing. It is not enough just to have legendary tactics. After all, thousands of people have studied the methods Alexander the Great used to conquer the known world…but no one has been able to use them to achieve the same outcome.

This is why GURUS Salespeople are leaders by default. They are inspired by things beyond themselves and their immediate wants. They can look in the mirror and honestly say…

"I am legend!"

Until you are inspired by something bigger, bolder and brighter than your bank account or ego, you will always be playing smaller than your potential.

The true point of inspiration is that you break through the bullshit of your pre-programmed limiting beliefs that tell you what you are capable of doing. The truth is that you are limitless!

Bruce Lee said, "Use no way as way. Have no limitation as limitation." This is the essence of selling big, which is the only way to do high end sales. Your personal drive must surpass the level of game you play. And…

High end sales is the biggest game in the world!

Do you desire to step onto the pro field?

If NO, then stop reading now.

If YES, then let's crank things up a notch!

☑ DO… Get Rich by Association

I want you to think about two old sayings. "Misery loves company" and "It's lonely at the top."

One of my mentors relies heavily on doing in-depth analyses of salespeople before designing coaching or training for them. He says he regularly finds salespeople who have all the tools and all the opportunities and still aren't living up to their potential. This is because they always have a peer group that is the same as them in terms of accomplishment.

They have friends, family and spouses who spend more time talking about their problems and why the world isn't fair than focusing on solutions. This is great if you want to be lower middle class and hang with the gang at the bar, but it ain't going to help you for squat if you want to be a legendary high end salesperson.

In order to become who you desire to be you must create an atmosphere around yourself that will facilitate the necessary changes in your attitude. And your personal atmosphere is created by the real, tangible items around you.

Physics shows us that there are things that are lighter than air and float or can create upward draft and fly. However, if you put too much weight on something it will come crashing back to the earth. So, we must lose unnecessary weight to maintain upward movement. And one of the heaviest items of all is people.

People can be damn heavy!

So, if you want to maintain you upward movement, you must maintain the right atmosphere around you. That means cutting off the people who weigh you down.

Now you've probably heard this advice before and determined that your current circle of friends and family are up to snuff. However, if you are reading this book, you're obviously wrong. You're very kind…but also wrong.

When we care about people and they care about us we simply believe that they are good to have around. We gloss over them when evaluating potential folks to remove from our lives. The problem is that we are doing them and ourselves an injustice.

You see, if I can't help you rise up and you can't help me rise up, then we will always be stuck at the same level staring at each other. At least if we break free of each other we have a shot at rousing ourselves enough to rise up.

So you have to look at your list again and be willing to cut lovingly AND mercilessly. It is always best for both of you. This goes for friends, family and even spouses and grown children.

When your children are young they deserve every chance and all the attention you can give them.

Now, I know that most people will automatically begin to protest this idea, especially when it comes to close family members. The fear is that if you cut yourself off from one or two family members the rest of the family may side with them and you'll lose all your family members. Possibly, but I doubt it. And…

If your family is so petty, you are better off without them!

Of course there is still hesitation. I know how it feels because I went through it too.

Shortly before writing this book I broke ties with a **very** close family member. It was difficult, but it needed to be done. I had stayed in communication with them because of their biological connection to me, until I realized that…

Biology was screwing with my mentality.

So I cut! I now have a **huge** weight off my shoulders and out of my mind.

And, in case you think this goes against being **genuine**, ask yourself if enduring someone else's **genuine** negativity is **genuinely** helping you or them? I rest my case.

How-To: Cut Negative People Out of Your Life

Evaluate your list of people and ask these questions…

1. Does this person have aspirations that far exceed their current status or are they "satisfied"?

2. Do they actively work toward those aspirations in a structured and consistent manner or do they "do things when they can"?

3. Do they talk positively about the future or do they complain about the present?

4. Do they encourage you to go for things that are beyond you right now or do they tell you to scale your hopes back so you're not "disappointed"?

5. Would you say this person is a role model for you in any area of your life?

6. Do you like to introduce this person to other people you know?

7. Has this person set and achieved quality goals before – in either life or business?

8. Do you feel lighter or heavier when this person is around you?

You must do this process for anyone you visit with more than once every six months. Some people you will be able to easily phase out. Some will take more to disconnect with. In the case of some family members, you may not be able to sever ties, but you at least need to minimize contact as much as possible.

Now, as we know, nature abhors a vacuum. So if you don't consciously set a new level of friends that you desire to associate with, you will seek out the same type of people you currently associate with by default. This is why stage two is FILL.

Imagine being able to be friends with anyone you desire. Who would you choose?

Be careful what you wish for, because you will get it.

How-To: Fill Your Life with Positive People

You must examine who to bring in as carefully as you did who to cut out. Ask yourself these questions…

1. What qualities or skills do I seek to increase in myself?

2. What income level do I desire to attain?

3. What subjects and activities interest me? (It can be something you do now or something you'd like to do)

4. What feelings about myself and my life do I want to feel on a regular basis?

5. What kind of people live the lifestyle I want to live?

6. Where do the people I'd like to be like congregate?

7. What do those people look for in a friend?

8. What can I offer – of myself, my experience, my connections, etc – to those people that they will appreciate?

Obviously, you should add to or edit the questions as best serves you. The important thing is that you do this because it is arguably the greatest gift you will ever give yourself. This *is* freedom!

Now answer the questions in as much detail as possible. Be honest, and do not hold back! This entire exercise is about breaking your boundaries, not reinforcing them!

Once you have your answers, find the fastest and easiest ways into your new friend-zone, like taking culinary classes, borrowing your neighbor's driver (golf club) and hitting some balls at the local driving range or asking your (remaining) friends or colleagues who they know who fits your criteria and seeing if they will introduce you.

You may end up with fewer friends for a while, but the ones you have will be far more inspirational for you and they will ultimately allow you to create a lifestyle that will be as rich with friend opportunities as it is with sales opportunities.

☑ DO... Mental Preparation, Not Mantras

I spent most of my late 20's and early 30's engaged in personal development. I had a mantra for virtually every aspect of my life.

In my mid-30's I met the first of my GURUS mentors and he showed me that mantras don't work!

For those of you out there who don't agree with me, let me put it another way...

Mantras don't work!

If mantras worked as intended (say it and it's true), then you should be able to sell anything to anyone simply by going up to them and saying, "This widget will make you richer" or some variation thereof.

Of course sales doesn't work that way. If you went and told people that your product or service did (something extraordinary) without any set up, they'd simply say "bullshit."

This is exactly what your mind says to mantras.

Let's examine a typical mantra.

Mantra: I am a great salesperson!

Your Mind: Bullshit!

Mantra: I am a great salesperson!

Your Mind: Bullshit x 2!

Mantra: I am a great salesperson!

Your Mind: Bullshit x 3, and I am going to wander now, since you are boring me!

Your mind, just like a client's during a sale, needs to change perspective before it will accept anything new. So, how do we change perspective in our minds? The same way we do with a client...ask questions!

Think about this: "I am a great salesperson" versus "What parts of my sales process am I really skilled at?"

Now your mind has to go and find answers. But, in order to find those answers, your mind first has to accept that you *are* skilled at some parts of your sales process. So, as it looks for and finds those answers…

It automatically creates and reinforces the confidence you desire.

This is why a few seconds of questions is far more powerful than hours of mantras.

Here are some more to try out…

- What do I love about what I sell?

- What feeling can I focus on creating today in my clients? (Like "excitement")

- What skill/data can I study that will broaden my horizons as a person and give me more in common with my clients?

- Who can I help in my sales team to improve their ability by teaching them something I do very well?

- What is lovable about me?

As you can see, these questions engage the mind, instead of boring it or telling it something it doesn't believe.

You will see this same thinking appear when we get into the actual sales process with clients, because it works!

☑ DO… Program Yourself While You Sleep

Ask anyone and they will tell you that there is something, usually a lot of things, they'd like to change about themselves. High end salespeople normally have several skills or characteristics they'd like to improve or acquire…

And several they'd like to bury in a shallow grave.

In making a personal change the challenge is for the new behavior to cross the threshold from the conscious mind to the unconscious mind. This is why most high end salespeople use mantras, self improvement CDs, notes to themselves, etc. These techniques either don't work or work so slowly they are almost useless.

Short of deep hypnosis, GURUS Salespeople know that the easiest way to bridge the conscious / unconscious gap is to program the change when the two minds meet naturally…at bedtime.

Research has shown that suggestions that people give themselves as they lay in bed and drift to sleep have a high retention and activation rate in the mind. This is because what you are thinking about before you go to sleep is what the mind will work on as you sleep.

Sleep programming is quite easy and very fun! Before you begin, make sure you know what you want to change, and make sure that you create some kind of measurement of your current ability level that you can refer back to at a later time.

How-To: Program Yourself While You Sleep

1. Get completely ready for bed, lay down and turn off the light.

2. In your mind, see yourself in third person having the skill or attribute you'd like to have. You can see it as a movie or picture; either is fine. (Example: Engaging people easily in conversation)

3. Maintain the picture and feel what it feels like to have that skill

now. Make sure you really *feel* the joy of having it now somewhere in your body.

4. Maintain the picture and the feeling and now give yourself (out loud or in your head) a description of what you want. Then say it again slightly differently. Then say it two more times, again slightly differently each time. (Example: "I want to engage people easily in conversation. I want to be a great conversationalist. I want to speak easily with new people. I want to be able to talk to anyone fearlessly.")

Now maintain the picture and the feeling until your mind disperses them naturally. Don't fight to hold them. The mind knows what it is doing.

Repeat this process every night for up to one month.

At the end of one month go back and measure your skill level against the level you gave yourself one month before. You will be pleasantly surprised with the improvement.

NOTE: Obviously this is for training yourself to get better at skills you already technically understand, like conversation or cold calling. You can't use this to learn skills that require actual training, like a new CRM software system or the technical specs for new products you sell. There are some things that still require "hitting the books."

☑ DO... Jump into Mistakes

In the realm of sales, mistakes are often looked upon as a curse to be avoided. So many sales managers rage about them and so many salespeople fear them that they have become taboo.

I used to be the same way. I feared making mistakes because I thought they would always have huge ramifications. But, as several of my GURUS mentors taught me...

Mistakes are the ONLY way for you to create the sales you desire!

It is impossible to go into any sales situation with all the answers – or any answers for that matter. Yet, many salespeople try to do just that. They try to be perfect before walking in the door. This leads to them hesitating to do meetings or get on the phone to make lead calls until they have their "pitch" and subsequent follow-ups down pat.

This drive for perfection only creates procrastination.

This ultimately slows down the entire sales process because every step that should flow swiftly and naturally is put off in the pursuit of a ridiculous standard – perfection – which can never be met.

Therefore, simply by allowing yourself to make mistakes in every forum – on the phone, with clients, in presentations – you will increase the amount of effort you put out. More effort equals more results. More results equals more feedback. More feedback equals more adjustment, and more adjustment equals more positive outcomes.

As we discussed earlier, feedback and adjustment are the vital parts in the creation of sales success – in this case more sales under your belt per month or year.

As one of my GURUS Mentors says, "action has its own innate intelligence." This means that you must act in order to be intelligent. Yet most people mistakenly believe they will get "intelligent" by *avoiding* action. It is more true to say that…

Inaction is innately ignorant!

So, the next time you are going to do something in your sales process and you hesitate because of what is going on in your head, like a little voice chattering away that you're about to make a mistake, smile and jump in knowing that you are about to close more sales faster!

☑ DO… Listen to the Voices in Your Head

Invariably as we go through our days we hear "voices" in our head. Even the most Zen of us still hear the voices.

These voices tend to appear when we have choices to make. There is usually the choice we would like to make and the choice – usually inaction or backing down – that the voice would like us to make.

Most salespeople try to tough it out and ignore the voice or yell at it in their heads until it goes away.

Of course, as one of my GURUS mentors used to drill into my head, "What you resist persists." So if you ignore or run-over the voice it will come back to haunt you again and again.

Here's the funny thing. The subconscious mind – where the voices come from – only wants to serve us. It does so even when it is going against what we ultimately want. And it will not stop until it has been heard and dealt with. So the easiest thing is to listen to it and deal with it.

Example: You have been dealing with a client who seems to love you or hate you every other time you call. You have to call him to go over the paperwork and hopefully get a signed deal, but this will be a "hate" call based on the pattern thus far.

Your little voice is screaming for you to do anything *but* make the phone call. And when you can't take the screaming anymore you decide to deal with it.

"What positive outcome are you trying to get for me?" You ask your little voice, remembering that it is there to *serve* you.

"I don't want you to lose the deal!" The voice fires back.

"Do you think I will *get* the deal by *not* calling?" You reply.

"Well…no," the voice says sheepishly.

"So I have to make the call, don't I?" You ask.

"Yes, you do." The voice agrees.

"Can you support me in this?" You start. "Could you possibly put better pictures in my mind and a more relaxed feeling in my body so I can be more at ease when I make this call?"

"Yes. I can do that." The voice responds.

Of course, this is a simplistic conversation I've laid out. Nonetheless, you can see how the process works.

And, in case you're thinking, "This is ridiculous. I'd just be talking to myself. It's all imaginary…"

What the hell do you think you were doing anyway?

All the times you tell your mind to "shut up" you're talking to it. This way, you're being kinder, taking control and creating the outcome you need.

☑ DO… Go AWOL on a Regular Basis

High end sales could just as easily be called "high pressure sales." It is a level of sales where burnout can happen very easily.

In the day-to-day drive to close deals and increase profits and commissions, salespeople can easily overlook the single most important, and always utilized, tool of their sales arsenal…their bodies.

GURUS Salespeople know that it is more productive and profitable to…

Pay attention to yourself first and your sales second.

A salesperson can easily fill every day of their lives with steps in the sales process…lead generation, meetings, follow-ups, contract review, etc. There is no shortage of work that can be done. And most sales managers will talk more freely about where their team members are falling behind than where they are succeeding, which creates an ongoing illusion that the deadline and goal is always out of reach.

The truth is that the "deadline" is inside you. You can easily be the death of your sales career by allowing yourself to burn out in the pursuit of ever-moving milestones and expectations. Therefore, it is vitally important for you to be able to gauge your own energy level and, as needed, go and recuperate regardless of what day it is or what your boss wants.

In the military, when a solider leaves without permission it is called going AWOL (Absent Without Official Leave). You need to engage the corporate version of this...except that you have the option of calling in sick and avoiding a court-martial.

When you are rested you will see the world through de-stressed eyes. You will be able to gain access to your relaxed state which gives you access to your higher level thinking, which is the thinking you want to be able to access when talking with clients and handling your boss.

So, don't be afraid to go AWOL now and then to maintain your health and healthy sales.

☑ DO... Maintain Your Sales Machine

Your body is your sales machine. And, like all machines, it needs fuel and regular maintenance to stay functional. Imagine leaving your car sitting in the garage for a year untouched and then trying to drive it on a 1,000-mile road trip. You'd be sitting in a tow truck real fast.

All of my GURUS mentors pay close attention to what they eat and how they exercise.

Now, I am not a dietician or a medical doctor. So I will not be giving you specific advice about what to eat or how to exercise your body. What I will tell you is that you would be well advised to do what all the great health specialists I know told me to do...research for yourself.

There are many factors that affect our food and exercise choices, including age, gender, preexisting conditions, family histories, blood type, allergies, etc. and, if you do nothing else, you should become well acquainted with the best foods for your body chemistry and the best exercises for your body type and start on them both now.

I should know....

At the ripe old age of 35 I had a heart attack!

And I was at the gym exercising when it happened! Now *that* is irony!

Long story short, all of my arteries were 99% open, except for one little area, about a millimeter wide, where it was 99% closed with plaque. And that little blockage almost cost me my life.

After I was released from the hospital I began to study everything I could on heart conditions, cholesterol, blood types, body types, etc. I realized that my exercising was fine, but the foods I was eating, even though supposedly healthy, weren't.

I have since changed almost everything I do for my health. I am now more energized and in better shape. And as a by-product, my focus and thinking have also improved, which are the key elements everyone needs in high end sales.

And, in case you think this section was just pointless "be healthy" babbling, remember that...

You will die!

So focusing on "wealthy" without the "healthy" may mean more money in the bank, but it also means a lot less time to enjoy it.

☑ DO... Read as Little as Possible

This may sound incredibly hypocritical to throw into the middle of a business book, but I have to say it...

You shouldn't read most business books.

It's not that most business books are good or bad. It is simply that most of the words in most business books are unnecessary.

If you have attended high school or college you have held a text book or two in your hands. Invariably the books had a lot of writing in them, but some words and sections were more important than others. "Read the stuff in bold" was my motto through most of school.

Now, I will admit that I did not graduate top of my class in either high school or college. But, I will also tell you that many of my academically decorated classmates are now middle managers at fast food restaurants. Nothing against them, but...

Being able to memorize stuff and regurgitate it on tests doesn't equal a million $$$ paycheck!

As a matter of fact, the false belief that "I have to know everything that is written here" can destroy your ability to really *use* the information in front of you.

Now, in the realm of business books we have an added wrinkle – author opinion. You see, when most people write business books they will portray it as "this is reality" as opposed to "this is *my* reality."

Basically, if you really read every word the author writes it is very easy to fall into group think with them and buy *their* self-limiting beliefs. Even the most successful billionaire who writes a book has some kind of limiting beliefs...

After all, he is ONLY a billionaire.

If he is so good, why isn't he a trillionaire?

So, since there is not much in the way of useful information in most business books, and we don't want to get caught up in believing that the author is right, one of my GURUS mentors created a quick system to read and use business books to their fullest advantage, while taking very little time.

How-To: Do the Need Read

1. Read the table of contents and select which chapters potentially have information or techniques you'd like to learn. Most books have chapters filled with stuff you already know or they have a lot of repetitive information.

2. Go to the chapter you want to learn from and read the first paragraph. Then go to the last page of the chapter and read the last paragraph. This gives you the basic beginning and end of the author's thought.

3. Review the chapter and look for the highlighted tactics, techniques, tips, diagrams, etc. Then, on a separate piece of paper or on your computer, write down the technique, tip, etc. in an abbreviated form so you have the basics of it.

4. Once you have completed your lists from the book, go back and review them. For each one decide if it makes sense to you, applies to your situation and would help your sales activity performance.

5. If necessary, add, delete or edit the tactic, technique, etc. however you see fit. Then test it out and see how it works for you. Remember that the way it worked for the author is not necessarily how it will work for you.

Ultimately this is all about how you *feel* with the technique. It is far more important that you feel good about using the tactic and that it helps you. If it made sense in a book, but doesn't work, what good is it?

I'd recommend this for *almost* every business book. There are exceptions of course, and I personally hope you'll make this book one of those exceptions…but you always have to do what is best for you!

SECTION TWO

How do <u>GURUS</u> get more leads?

BE DO SALE

Chapter 5
<u>BE</u> a Creator

So at this point you have searched your soul and found your genuine self. You know that you really love or respect that which you have decided to sell. You have the ability to amplify yourself and your enthusiasm and you can handle any of the negative self-talk that your well-intentioned brain might throw at you.

And yet, you know as well as I do that you can feel wonderful and powerful all day long…but if you aren't bringing in new leads you aren't going to make new sales. Good thing that lead generation is a staple of the GURUS System.

The first U in GURUS stands for Unique Sales Persona. Your Unique Sales Persona is required for you to do effective lead generation. But before you can get around to doing lead generation you need the structure in which to do it. So we will explore how GURUS <u>create</u> the best structure for lead generation and all their sales activities.

☑ DO… Bypass Goal Setting

Goal setting is a billion-dollar industry. It is interwoven into training for salespeople, m is means that every desired outcome becomes a goal.

So, by this definition, if I want to make myself a hamburger for lunch it has the same "goal value" as wanting to take my company from $5MM in revenue to $40MM in revenue in three years. Somehow those two "goals" don't seem to be of the same caliber…at least to me.

So, let's establish what goals are. Goals are those way far out there things that can only be accomplished if you have to go through a good deal of effort and personal change (i.e. breaking comfort zones), and achieve many shorter-term desired outcomes to get to them.

Therefore, our hamburger is not a goal but just a meal.

Another issue with goals is their specificity. Like anything else in life…

Your perspective on your goals changes with your distance from them.

Example: One of my GURUS mentors tells the story of a vacuum parts company he dealt with back in the 80's.

The company was doing about $8MM in sales when my mentor went to work for them as a VP of Sales. The owner's "goal" was to get to $25MM in sales in three years. So, my mentor set about making that happen.

After two years they hit $15MM in sales. However, to reach more retailers and resellers to sell more products, they had to spend more on travel for the sales team, advertising and co-advertising, production, etc. Understandably, even though they were making more in sales, they were keeping less money. Plus, the owner was working longer hours to handle everything.

My mentor talked with the owner and found that he had wanted to reach $25MM because he thought that was enough to hire people to run the operation for him and he could be an "absentee owner" instead of "hands-on" every day.

At this point they worked out what numbers the owner would need to retire, which was his real concern since he was already in his 50's. Within six months they had sold the company to a competitor. The owner got a sizeable buyout but my mentor also negotiated a revenue share of future profits for him as well. So the owner got to retire, live well and have more money than he had been planning on.

My mentor got a nice bonus for helping with the sale and, after it was seen how wisely he handled sales and negotiating, he was whisked up the corporate ladder of his new employer.

As you can see, distance changes perspective. So the answer is to set big goals, without limitations. Don't say, "I want to get up to $5MM in sales annually by doing XYZ tactic." Instead, say something like, "I want to generate $100MM in income annually" without specifying *how*. Then examine every possible strategy to get there.

> ## *Most people make the mistake of making their strategies for reaching goals into goals as well.*

This is problematic in that it again mixes up goals, strategies, steps, tactics, techniques, etc.

What you really want is to set achievable outcomes.

☑ DO... Control Outcomes

When sales VPs or sales managers talk about the "strategy" for the month, quarter, year, etc., they get into a very gray area. This is because they are again mixing things up. Goal, strategy, tactic, plan, technique, steps, etc. get all mixed together and used interchangeably.

> ## *This is why you can have a "strategy" clearly laid out for you and still not know what to do!*

One of the GURUS mentors specializes in creating sales strategies for *Fortune 100* companies. He explained the breakdown to me this way...

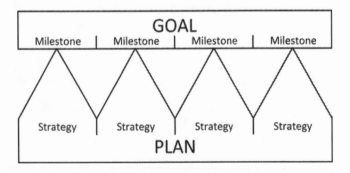

The <u>Goal</u> is first. It is the big, bright, out there dream.

The Goal is broken up into <u>Milestones</u> which help to measure progress to the Goal.

The Plan is the semi-fluid, semi-solid path to achieve the Goal.

The Strategy is the shorter-range piece of the Plan that is more solid and used to reach a Milestone.

The Tactic is the pieces into which the Strategy breaks down.

A Step is the breakdown of the Tactic.

Steps then have to broken into actual Activities.

Finally, the Technique is the *way* you do each Activity.

Now, it's very nice that you understand how these pieces all fit together. But that still doesn't help you because, at the end of the day, all people really want is Outcomes. So, let's talk about outcomes.

There are two types of outcomes: Those you can control and those you can't.

You *can* control having tied shoelaces. You *can't* control tomorrow's weather.

The big monkey wrench that many folks allow to grow and fester in their technique-to-goal chains is counting on uncontrollable outcomes. This is why so many people fail to reach big goals.

Example: Let's take two sales teams. We'll call them A and B.

Team A wants to "close" 100 new clients this month. Right now they are averaging 86 per month.

Team B decides to have each salesperson spend an extra hour doing lead generation calls per day. Right now they do two hours per day. They are also getting 86 new clients per month.

Team A's desire for 100 new customers may be achievable, but it is completely uncontrollable. This is because it hasn't been broken down into controllable pieces. It is simply a poorly-thought-out "goal."

Sadly, this is how many sales teams do their "planning." The sales manager sets out a desired number and leaves it up to the salespeople to figure out how to achieve it. Because the sales manager is confusing a goal with what should be an activity, he is misleading his team and doing far more harm than good.

Team B's decision is easily achievable and wholly controllable. By adding an extra hour per day to their lead generation calling, they are increasing it by 50%. So, if lead generation calls are producing the current 86 clients per month, we can predict with some confidence that they will increase their new client level to about 129 per month within a month (86 + 50% increase = 129).

So, the lesson here is to examine all of your goals, plans, etc. and make sure that they are broken down into steps and activities. This way you will not be stuck in that "what do I do now?" zone that so many salespeople fall into regularly, which kills energy, confidence and sales.

☑ DO... Smarket Yourself

"People will pay more for the experience" – Simon Sinek
"Business is really easy. People make it hard." – Erik Luhrs

Unstoppable sales growth is simple. Yet 99.9% of companies screw it up!

Don't believe me?

Well, does your company have a marketing department? Sure it does. And does that department have a budget and staff? Yes again! And is the marketing department sending you and your sales teammates so many new leads that you can't even handle them all? That would be a big NO!

Now, I could go off on a tangent about how to fix your company's marketing department and system...but that isn't the point of this book! And you most likely work for the sales department, so let the marketing department get its own book!

This means that you and your teammates in the sales department have to generate your own leads, which means you have to do your own marketing. And the ridiculous thing is that your company keeps funding the marketing department!

As long as the folks in marketing put together some brochures or rent trade show booths or blow millions on hiring advertising companies to really screw things up, they get praised. But if you don't make your numbers this month, you're in trouble!

See, the last time I checked...

Marketing's job is to drive leads to the sales team!

But this seems to be long forgotten in today's age of 'spend poorly and blame liberally.'

Why is this? Because your MSCEF is broken!

MSCEF stands for *Marketing to Sales to CRM Experience Funnel™*. This is the system that all companies dream of having, think they have...and desperately need to have...but don't.

The funnel is so simple to do right and so consistently done wrong.

You see, it's *all* an experience. When a prospect has their first experience with your company, they need to have that experience enhanced and built upon. That is how the funnel is supposed to work.

BE DO SALE

Example: Your marketing department puts an ad in an in-flight magazine to sell your consulting services. The prospect sees the ad and has a first impression and opinion of your company. The ad then drives them to visit your company's website.

So our prospect goes to the website when they are back in their office. The website either aligns with and enhances the prospect's experience with your company or it doesn't, which breaks the prospect's experience and they flow out of the funnel.

But let's say that your marketing department has enough of an aligned theme and message to get the prospect from the magazine ad to the website to a webinar, after which they request a follow-up call from a representative.

Now the sales department steps in. If there is alignment between the marketing department and the sales department, then the client has a smooth transition and their experience is built upon and enhanced.

But if the marketing and sales departments are in a constant turf war with each other or just ignore each other, which is usually the case, and there is no alignment in message or experience between the two departments, then the client will again slip out of that crack in the funnel.

The same basic issues go on down the line through the CRM department.

The client's <u>experience</u> is the most important thing.

And it seems to be the last thing on the minds of those who handle the funnel at any given point. This is why most companies screw up their limitless sales potential, because they haven't created a solid MSCEF for their people. And therefore everyone suffers: The client, the company and you.

In today's economic environment if I told you that corporations were wasting billions of dollars a year on buying nothing you'd think I was insane. After all, every company is looking for how to shore up its accounts and drive up its bottom line.

Yet, as I have just laid out for you, millions of companies spend billions of dollars on marketing every year for absolutely no results!

How do I know this? Because the salespeople from these companies call me and ask me how to get leads their marketing department can't!

This happens because company leaders think that if they aren't spending money on putting the company name everywhere online, in print, and on the air they might lose "top of mind" status. Of course, just because you are top of my mind doesn't mean you'll get my bottom dollar.

Again, this situation arises because of a break in the *Marketing to Sales to CRM Experience Funnel*™.

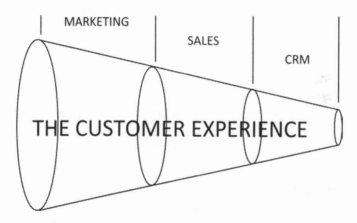

As you can see, the front of the funnel is marketing. Marketing is supposed to pull people in so the sales team can turn them into customers. However, most marketing departments today simply waste money on advertising agencies or on their own ideas for getting the "brand" out there.

And of course, this breakdown between marketing and sales leaves the CRM portion of the funnel virtually helpless.

The most important thing for you to understand is that if the marketing department won't get the people into the funnel, then the salespeople (you) will have to.

So it is vitally important that salespeople learn how to market themselves or become "Smarketers" as I lovingly call them.

Salesperson who can Market = Smarketer.

As a Smarketer you have only one mission: Increase the ROI of your lead generation efforts!

Though there are many ways to do lead generation, there are only three ways to Increase its ROI...

I. Improve the performance of your current tactic(s)

II. Increase the amount you do of your current tactic(s)

III. Add more tactics

Honestly, because there are so many ways to do lead generation, each way has its own unique improvement factors. However, so you can get started, I have put together a basic process for you to use as a guide.

How-To: Improve Your Current Lead Generation Tactics

1. Select which tactic you wish to improve (Example: Lead generation calls, sales letters, blog conversions, etc.)

2. Break the tactic down into its steps. (Example: Lead generation calls break down into the list you use, the time of day you call, the days you call, the opening you use, the body or script you use, the rapport you can build, the call to action you offer, etc.)

3. Break the step down into its activities. (Example: The opening you use breaks down into your tone of voice, your speed of speech, the words you say, etc.)

4. Choose one activity you wish to improve. (Example: The words you say)

5. Gauge your current success level with the technique you use in that activity. (Example: Three out of ten people listen to your opening and don't hang up)

6. Create no less than two and no more than five new versions of the technique to test. (Example: "Hello I'm calling about your software

needs" or "Are you looking for new software?" or "When was the last time you measured how much money you lose per minute on outdated software?", etc.)

7. Test each version equally. (Example: Try your three new openings for one hour each per day for three days, varying which you use first, second and third)

8. Compare the conversion ratio of each new opening and use the one that converts best.

You can now take this same process and use it on other techniques in other activities.

Ultimately this will improve the overall ROI of your lead generation tactics. Yes, it will take time and effort to test and improve all your techniques and activities, but since the only other choice is to keep doing what you're doing, getting the same results and continuing to be frustrated, I think you'll be happy you made the investment.

How-To: Do More of Your Current Lead Generation Tactics

Yes, this is pretty obvious, but it needs to be said. Once you have a tactic that works, do more of it!

The only caveat is that you have to make sure that you are not taking away resources from other tactics/activities that produce better results or are necessary to complete sales.

How-To: Add More Lead Generation Tactics

Yes, again, this is pretty obvious! But I would be remiss to not formally address it.

Once you have fully leveraged or at least gotten an existing lead generation tactic to an acceptable level, you simply add a new one.

The caveat here is that you should make sure to adhere to a budget and test your new efforts. Test using small dollars, improve them, then invest big.

☑ DO... Make Things Smaller and Smaller

Several years ago, when I was still doing general business coaching, I tried everything to get clients. I went to networking events every morning (Oh, what awful eggs!). I went to events at night. I sent fax blasts. I did e-mail blasts. I hit up everyone for referrals. I sent marketing letters. I did it all!

Of course, when I would actually speak to someone, like at the networking events, they would always ask me what I did and who I did it for. I babbled out something about "improving small businesses." I got polite responses, but no leads.

Finally, one of my GURUS mentors told me that I had to niche down my target market. I thought I had. After all, I was after "small businesses."

My mentor informed me that *everyone* was after small businesses. And since there were millions of small businesses, I had to be just a *little* more specific. I have since taken that lesson to heart!

How-To: Niche-Down Your Target Market

1. Break down potential clients by the basic demographics – industry, annual sales, staff size, production volume, market share, etc.

2. Eliminate anyone that would have difficulty paying for what you have to offer. If you're left with only one group, all the better!

3. Divide the remaining groups into...

    a. *Prospects Who Desperately Want or Need What I Sell*

    b. **Prospects Who Might Need Some Time to Buy**

4. Now divide Prospects **Who Desperately Want or Need What I Sell** into...

    a. **Prospects whose industry or issue I have experience in**

  b. *Prospects whose industry or issue I don't have experience in*

5. Look for any way to further subdivide *Prospects Whose Industry or Issue I Have Experience In*, such as sales volume or their geographic location.

You should be left with a substantially smaller list, which means you are ready for the flip side…

☑ DO… Choose as You Beg

After some time working with my first set of niche criteria I was getting more sales. However, I regularly found myself working with folks that I did not really enjoy or who gave me a hard time or who just seemed to bring me down.

At this point one of the GURUS mentors I was training with told me that I had only done half of the niching I needed to do. He said, "You have decided who you're qualified to work with, but you haven't decided who is qualified to work with you."

He went on to explain that as long as I was willing to deal with anyone that had a pulse and checkbook I was doomed to get clients I did not enjoy.

I was still whoring myself for money!

And since I was doing well financially, it was to time to raise my standards by finally setting them.

I then devised standards my prospects had to meet to have the privilege of working with me. I present my process for creating your standards below. As always, you may use or change it as you see fit.

How-To: Devise Your Minimum Standards for Clients

1. Choose an attitude you want the client to possess. Do you want your dealings with them to be fun, short, easy, challenging, mind-blowing, etc?

2. Choose a passion level the client must have. Do you want your clients to be passionate about what they do? Just profitable? Only concerned with profits? Working for a greater cause, like poverty eradication, etc?

3. Choose an appreciation level from the client. Does the client gain value from just your presence? Or do you want them to make you work for their respect? Or do they just appreciate price and quantity, etc?

4. Choose a belief alignment for the client to have. Do they believe what you do? Are they Catholic or Jewish? Do they vote Republican or Democrat? Do they think the Dodgers should have stayed in Brooklyn? What are the core beliefs you want your prospects to share with you?

5. Choose an action orientation level for the client. Are they highly motivated and looking to grow their business? Do they just want the product now, so they can keep moving? Are they clueless and just hoping for a miracle? Are they lazy and want everything done for them, etc?

With this process you are designing a friend, not a client. You will feel who is worth pursuing and who is worthy of buying from you, because you now know what you expect from them.

☑ DO... Ask Before You Receive

Okay, so now you have defined the people you want to smarket to and who has the right stuff to buy from you.

Of course, none of that means squat if you don't get anyone's attention or interest. The only way to get attention and interest is by creating some kind of message that has immediate meaning to your niched target market.

This is another point where many salespeople drop the ball.

They simply decide, based on their own "experience," what their clients want or need to hear. Then they proceed to blow money on business cards, brochures, LinkedIn ads, etc. that send out generalized come-ons like "We'll help you cut your operations costs by at least 10%."

That is benefit-aimed messaging. It used to work when there was little or no competition. But nowadays, if your competitors can say the same thing, then your claim means nothing and will be ignored.

Don't worry. I did this too, so I know how it is. Thankfully, three of my GURUS mentors are behind-the-scenes experts in marketing and messaging. They aren't any big-name experts you'd know…but they're the guys who made the big-name experts you know!

The single most important lesson that I learned by observing them is that…

What you think is important to your clients is useless.

The only thing that matters, and works in terms of messaging, is what clients tell you is important to them.

So you need to research and discover what your niched target market wants and needs to hear from you. The best way to do this is in an interview / research format; as if you were writing a white paper or book.

How-To: Research Your Niched Target Market for Message Design

1. Determine what specific problem you want to help your target market with. Do you want to be an IT hardware reseller to aircraft manufacturing companies? Do you want to sell cost-reduction consulting services to CFOs of financial firms? Do you want to be the yacht salesperson to the world's billionaires? You must know what specific problem(s) you want to help your prospects with.

2. Gather a list of people in your target market. This can be done through databases, such as InfoUSA or Dun & Bradstreet. It can also be done by asking your current contacts who they know that fits into your target market. You can also put out requests on sites like LinkedIn or HARO (helpareporter.com).

3. Design the questions to use in your interview. Use open questions up front. If you start asking highly specific questions immediately they will answer you, but you won't know if their answer describes an actionable pain for them.

4. Example: You can ask someone "what is your biggest IT expense?" and they'll answer, but that doesn't tell you if their IT costs are a big issue for them. They might be far more focused on the fact that their CEO is about to retire and they have no idea who is going to replace him

5. So you want to identify their biggest issue(s). If their biggest issue has to do with what you sell then continue. If not then end the conversation quickly. There is no point in trying to "steer" or "convince" people.

6. As the person answers your questions give each answer a corresponding pain level from 1 to 10. 1 being little pain and 10 being big pain. The scale is subjective and based entirely on how you feel about their answers. Listen to the strain – or lack thereof – in their voice, the speed with which they answer, etc. You will get a feeling from them that you can gauge.

7. Ask ever deeper and more specific questions until you feel you have hit a pain level between 5 and 7. At this point you will have the answers you need for the next DO.

Remember that the more interviews you do, the better off you'll be. Personally, I interview at least 50 different people from my niched target markets before beginning any kind of smarketing.

GURUS TWEAK: Once you reach level 5, 6 or 7 with the interviewee you can take your answers and end the interview there, or you can turn the conversation into a sales opportunity. Simply use some of the rapport-to-UBP processes we will be detailing later in the book.

This works because you already have credibility with the client. You are interviewing them and most people perceive that only "experts" interview people. You also have a certain level of rapport. It doesn't take much to engage them in exploring their UBP and engaging a full-on sales process.

☑ DO... Create a Pain-Problem Matrix

Now that you have interviewed people from your niched target market you will have a list of their problems.

At this point you want to create Pain-Problem Matrix using the information you have. The PPM is like any basic matrix you saw in high school math.

	Interviewee 1	Interviewee 2	Interviewee 3
1	increase sales	increase sales	increase sales
2			
3	stagnant growth		this tech is not vital
4		economy not helping	
5	finding clients at right time	no one sees need for IT now	no one buying
6	shorten sales cycle		shorten sales cycle
7		shorten sales cycle	
8	seeing creation used	get paid on time	
9			
10			Near bankrupt

The vertical axis represents levels of pain from 1 to 10. The horizontal axis represents the problems the interviewee had. The problems are ranked according to the pain level you perceived from the interviewee when they told you about them.

After all, one person might feel that the problem of "too much competition" causes them only shallow pain, like a level 2, while someone else may feel that "too much competition" causes them great pain, like a level 8. Again, you have to gauge their pain level as you talk to them.

As you can see from the example, you stack each interviewee's information next to the others'. Once you have interviewed a few dozen folks you will have a matrix that looks like the one above.

At this point you want start looking across your matrix at the levels 5 to 7. You are looking for problems that repeatedly show up between these two levels for multiple interviewees. Once you have identified a problem that repeatedly shows up between level 5 and level 7 for more than 25% of your interviewees…

You have a pain-problem that your niched target market will respond to!

Any problem that averages less than a level 5 pain is so shallow that it will be a generalized problem that everyone accepts, so talking about it in your message will just get you ignored. Anything deeper than a level 7 is usually personal to that individual, so designing a message around that will just confuse everyone else.

You now have several distinct problems that you can use in your messaging to get the attention of your niched target market!

You are ahead of 99% of the folks who do marketing for a living… Congratulations!

You'll see how the pain-problem matrix comes to life in the UBP section later on.

☑ DO... Double Cross Your Clients

"Exclusivity breeds desire." – Erik Luhrs

Whenever I talk to people other than my clients about niching down their target markets, they always agree with me. Then they go out and do the exact opposite. They have the same general message aimed at the same general audience. Essentially it is scattershot marketing.

Now, I believe that people do the best they can with the resources available to them. So I know that they aren't shooting themselves in the foot on purpose. They do it because some part of their brain tells them to keep trying to sell to everyone.

They are afraid that if they focus on one niche they will lose client opportunities. Of course, all of my GURUS mentors will tell you nothing could be farther from the truth.

Example: One of my mentors was hired as the salesperson for a small accounting firm in the Midwest in the early 1990's. The owners of the firm had done haphazard marketing and had no niched target market. They left it to my mentor to work a miracle.

My mentor examined the client base and saw that most of their clients were doctors. He went to the owners and said that he was going to focus on doctors to pursue as clients.

The owners were very nervous. They didn't like the idea of focusing solely on doctors because they feared they'd lose other types of businesses as possible clients. My mentor got a grudging "okay" from them.

Of course they didn't know that he was also lying to them.

My mentor did intend to focus only on doctors. But the owners thought he was going after all types of doctors. My mentor was actually going to focus on only one type of doctor, chiropractors. Had my mentor told the owners his full idea he never would have gotten the "okay."

Now, it was the early 1990's and the chiropractic field was literally exploding across America. At the same time chiropractors were fighting for credibility, since mainstream doctors still viewed them as con artists. So when my mentor came into their offices and said his firm specialized in accounting for chiropractors, they ate it up. They felt that someone was taking them seriously.

But it gets better! In six months my mentor increased the firm's business by over 30% just with chiropractors.

Then the second phase my mentor had planned took effect. The chiropractors were so pleased with the performance of the accounting firm, and the feeling of respect they got from working with the firm, that they began to tell their friends, families and clients about the firm.

Six months later they'd added another 45% of business simply by this process. And not once did they change their message about specializing in chiropractors. They simply said that they would "also" work with other people when the chiropractors' friends and clients called, as if the firm was making an exception in their case! Now they felt really special!

As you can see, people want great things regardless of whether or not they are the target market.

People are jealous of the good results of others.

This is the truth that drives The Double Cross Niche Process and The Triple Cross Jealousy Theory.

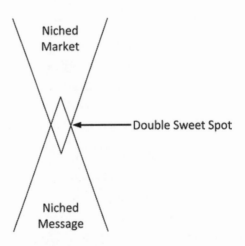

The highly niched-down focus on a target market aligns with the highly niched-down message aimed at that target market, creating a sweet spot. Everyone in that sweet spot now desires your product or service.

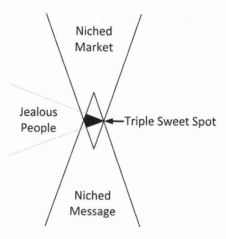

As these new clients have success with your solution their friends, colleagues, families, etc. see this success and want it as well. So now these non-targeted clients also seek you out. And you weren't even smarketing to them!

So, aiming at one niched market isn't only smart. It is also the fastest and easiest way to get the general audience you thought you'd lose by focusing on the one niche!

☑ DO... Stop Making Cold Calls

Cold calling. What a term, huh? A total turn-off for most salespeople. The name alone conjures up images of frozen wastelands bereft of life...or leads...or sales. Little wonder salespeople will find any excuse not to make these calls.

And I am in the same boat. I hate them too. So, I don't make them anymore. Now that doesn't mean that I don't occasionally pick up a phone and call someone I have never spoken to before in order to solicit business.

At this point you might be thinking that I just contradicted myself. But I didn't.

On those rare occasions when I do a lead generation call, the call is always HOT.

And oddly enough this idea was taught to me by one of the biggest GURUS mentors of all…God!

One day I was at home minding my own business and enjoying some pointless action movie because my wife had taken the kids out for the afternoon. I was drinking a beer and munching on some peanuts when the doorbell rang.

When I opened the door an overly well-dressed young man was standing there. I looked down and saw some literature in his hand and realized that he was with a division of the Christian faith that shall remain nameless.

Normally I would have made a quick excuse and closed the door. But there was something in his energy that stopped me.

He asked me about my religion and such, but unlike the mechanized, practiced speeches I usually heard from his counterparts, this guy interweaved his own thoughts and feelings. His passion for his lord was without doubt. And I realized he was standing at this doorway not for himself and not even really for me but because…

He had a message, a mission, that had to be delivered.

Although I did not convert that day I was incredibly impressed by the fact that he managed to have me keep my door open for several minutes without ever having to put his foot in between. And, had I been seeking a new direction in my own faith, this guy definitely would have gotten me to a meeting or two.

He was hot with the love of God!

He hadn't made a cold call at my door. He had made a burning hot call at my door!

So, when you are thinking about prospecting by phone, think about your higher calling. What do you love about what you sell? Why do you love what you sell? Why must that message be spread, regardless of who says yes? And why must it be spread NOW?

Truly get in touch with these feelings inside yourself and don't be surprised if you feel like a higher power is speaking through you when you pick up that phone!

☑ DO... Use the Internet to Steal

For my old-fashioned sales friends who say they don't need the Internet to market themselves, enjoy your limited potential! The Internet is not a fad. And it isn't going away.

Of course, to be fair, for my friends who think that they can master sales from behind a computer keyboard, enjoy your limited potential as well! You have to be around human beings to be like them and create sales with them.

The Internet is a tool, and it needs to be used well. The easiest way to use the Internet to increase sales is to have your own website and host your own blog. You can also do podcasts, write articles, host an Internet radio show, etc.

Sadly, few salespeople ever set up even a basic website.

And, for the few who do, most of those sites will sit idle and unchanged for years, which makes them useless.

Some salesperson will use the 'cut and paste' website their company gives them. These are the stock websites the company supplies and all the salesperson does is input a picture of themselves and their contact information. Other than that it looks exactly the same as all of their colleagues' sites.

In this way the site is nothing more than a business card or brochure...and you see how well those do for you in the real world! Do you think they will fare better in the virtual one?

The main point is that you need to create a presence on the internet and you need to consistently update it. This tends to be the most vexing issue for salespeople, and the one that stops them from really utilizing the

Internet. They all wonder, "what do I say after I have told people who I am and what I do?" They want to know how to create fresh content for their site or blog.

The answer is simple...Steal it!

No matter what you sell there are hundreds of "experts" in your industry who have websites, blogs, articles, books, etc. talking about any of the millions of aspects that have to do with what you sell.

Steal their stuff!

Now, understand that literally stealing their material and copying it word for word is plagiarism and that is illegal! So don't do that!

However, it is not illegal to read an article, have a different opinion or a different way of looking at the same idea and writing an article in your own words.

Many writers will tell you that there is only one story in the world and that every person merely tells it a different way. So, if that is true...

You are no better or worse than Stephen King, Tom Clancy or even Zig Ziglar.

A fast way to get started is to go to Google right now and type in your industry name followed by "blog" or "articles" and see what pops up. You will have unlimited material that you don't have to think up. You merely read and rewrite in your own words.

You will easily be able to update a blog on a regular basis and have new stuff for your visitors to read which keeps you relevant and starts to build your credibility, which we will explore in depth in the next chapter.

CHAPTER 6
<u>BE</u> A DIVIDER

Although it may be apparent by now, it is nonetheless worth clearly stating this point: In order to "conquer" your market you must first divide it. Divide and then you can conquer.

There is only so much dividing you can do in the planning stage, such as choosing demographics for your target market and setting up your own expectations from clients.

The more dramatic and meaningful way to really divide your target market is to do so through your actions. In this chapter we will discuss how to do just that.

☑ DO... Act like a Salebrity

WARNING: <u>Do not read this section unless you really want to increase your sales and, more importantly, are ready to make all the necessary changes in your life to do so!</u>

"Differentiate" is a big buzz word these days, and like all buzz words it has gone from obscure to overused very quickly. Also, like most buzzy concepts, it has been extrapolated and distorted to the Nth degree.

Most salespeople try to use a Unique Selling Proposition to differentiate themselves or what they sell. But...

The days of the Unique Selling Proposition are over.

Other salespeople tell me that their "quality" or "service" or "concern for the customer" is their differentiator. I just laugh because if these really made the difference, you could charge outrageous sums for your wares and get them so long as you provided quality service and had real compassion for your clients.

Obviously, there has to be a better differentiator. And there is.

It's called a Credibility and Authority Position.

Think about people like Brian Tracy and Zig Ziglar, the poster children for the perfect salesperson. They did not get to that status by remaining obscure sales reps in middle market or even *Fortune 500* companies. They got to where they are today by going beyond being anonymous salespeople to writing books, creating seminars and generally staking their claim to the banner of "guru" that they desired.

Now, imagine if Zig Ziglar started selling *IBM* consulting services right now. *IBM's* profits in that sector would go through the roof! Would it be because their consulting services had made a radical change in depth or value? No; it would be because a celebrity…or in this case a salebrity…was now talking about them.

This is the same reason that big companies hire spokespeople, like Tiger Woods for *Buick* or William Shatner for *Priceline*.

Their celebrity brings attention to the product.

Now, think about your company. If they could hire Tracy or Ziglar to sell for them, but did not have pay them more than the rest of their staff, do you think they'd do it? You're damn right they would! Without a second thought!

Of course, Ziglar and Tracy aren't available to sell for anyone but themselves at this point in time. And kudos to them for that. But the point is that the model works. Celebrity draws attention and allows that person to grow beyond the confines of obscurity and become a power player.

This is the surest and most profitable way for salespeople to differentiate themselves, to become salebrities.

GURUS go for Salebrity!

It is the only way to create omni-directional growth in your income and opportunities while still maintaining the "security" of a job.

And even better, your company truly wants you to create and raise your own salebrity brand...whether or not they know it...because it will ultimately raise their brand and profits too.

☑ DO... Profit Through Prolificacy

In order to claim your salebrity status you must become a thought leader.

Many salespeople will tell me that they have written an article or two and that they even have a blog they update "sometimes." Imagine if you did lead generation "sometimes." Do you think you'd have many clients?

You can't be a thought leader without a <u>continuous</u> stream of thoughts that <u>lead</u> people. To become a thought leader...

You must balance the quality of your thoughts with the quantity.

One of my GURUS mentors compares getting your message out to planetary physics.

"There are countless specks of dust, rocks, and asteroids floating out in space. When these things collide they get bigger. But it's not until they reach 500 miles wide that they are considered a planetoid. That's a lot of collisions!

"Only when something becomes a planetoid does it begin to have a gravitational pull that actually pulls other objects to it. So, if you want to pull prospects to you, you have to create a planet!"

What he was telling me was that I had to put so much content out there (dust, rocks, etc.) that collectively it would have enough mass to start *pulling* people to me.

Obviously, the quantity is ultimately up to you. You have to find a balance of how much you create and share versus how much your clients want to hear or see from you.

Personally, I believe that people who love you will love more and more of you. This is why I strive to create new material on a regular basis. But again this is up to you.

The big question in this process is the quality of your thoughts. Now "quality" doesn't really mean the spelling or grammar. It refers to the value of your thoughts to your target market.

Most salespeople who engage in this activity just take other people's ideas and regurgitate them.

This is why no one reads their articles or watches their videos.

There are only so many times you can read stuff like "How to Do Time Management" or "The Five Things to Look For Before Buying an IT Solution" before you gloss right over those kinds of titles.

Honestly, in order to get attention and build your salebrity brand you're going to have to piss some people off.

☑ DO... Speak to Both Ends at Once

I'm not very big on "sales pitches" or "silver bullet opening lines," because at best they get limited attention and at worst they annoy people. But if you're going to do it, do it right.

Many times, when drafting messages, be it for a sales letter, flyer, sales pitch or any type of marketing statement, salespeople tend to open with what they can *do* for the client.

Examples...

"We can wash your windows."

"Do you need a new sales manager?"

"The number one pest control company in New Jersey."

"We're the only company that offers free job boards."

This approach is based on the incorrect presumption that the client already knows exactly what they are looking for and is simply waiting until they see your material to take action.

In truth, clients have a gap in their minds about what has to be done to solve their situation, because if they didn't they would have solved it already. So...

All a client really knows is their current reality and their desired reality.

Current reality - This is how the client tells themselves on a daily, moment to moment basis what is wrong in their world.

Example: The client knows they have an ant problem in their house. So they set traps and use sprays for several months. But the ants keep coming back. That's their current reality. So, to speak to it you'd simply use an opening like, "Have you tried everything but those darn ants just keep coming back?"

That approach is speaking to **current** reality.

But speaking to current reality only gets their attention, so you have to also address **desired** reality.

Desired reality - This is the outcome they desire.

Example: Using our "ant" analogy again, we would lead with a statement like, "Have you tried everything but those darn ants just keep coming back? Would you like to open your cupboards and see only the food you put there, free of tiny intruders?"

This is the essence of Current and Desired Messaging.

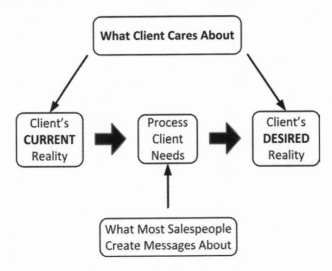

At this point the client's current and desired realities have been tapped. And they are open to hearing about the action steps (i.e. process) that will be required to get from one to the other.

Now you can talk about what you do with an audience that is ready to listen rather than one that is already gone.

☑ DO... Create the New USP - Unique Sales Persona

> *"How an individual salesperson is perceived is now more important than the products being offered or the company they represent."* – Tom Freese

Lots of salespeople ask me how to create a great USP. Of course they are asking me about creating a *Unique Selling Proposition*. As I mentioned previously, this type of USP is pretty much over. This because in today's marketplace if you can't say you are the *first* or *only* then your unique selling proposition isn't unique.

Also, since competitors are always looking for ways to copy, undercut and outdo you, the amount of time you have to be the *only* is limited and being *first* has little weight once a market is filled with "me too" competitors who will do it cheaper.

My GURUS mentors use another and far more powerful USP...the Unique Sales Persona. I call it the **New USP**!

You see, most folks engaged in high end sales have heard the advice that you should try to be as much like your desired clients as possible. You should dress like them. You should talk like them. You should walk like them. You should think like them. You should eat what they eat...You get the idea.

The only problem with that logic is that eventually you become so much like your client and every other salesperson they deal with that you no longer stand out.

That logic is the perfect recipe for camouflaging yourself!

This is great if you're hunting elk, but not so hot for getting the attention of a CEO.

So, what you must find is the point where you have enough in common with the client to enter their world and enough difference from the client so that you also stand out. The easiest way to do this is to be yourself...literally.

This is how personal branding begins. Personal branding is a by-product of being the authentic you.

Think about it. High level buyers are stalked by a herd of blue suit-wearing, corny joke-spewing salespeople with perfectly coiffed hair and one too many gold rings. They have become herd animals because they seek safety in the old logic. They have stopped being themselves in order to fit a role they think they're supposed to play.

They are fakes!

A great example of the power of the Unique Sales Persona is Zig Ziglar.

He likes to be well dressed and well groomed. And he also likes to carry his bible. And that's it! The bible drives his Unique Sales Persona. He can gesture with it. He can thump it. He can refer to it. He can do all sorts of things with it. But it is not a prop. It is his faith on display for all to see. He is speaking from his truth, not from an act.

So what about you?

Well, simply by wearing a suit that's perhaps green or beige you begin to break the visual monotony. By asking if they've seen the science fiction movie you went to last week, you break the verbal monotony. By wearing a rubber band around your wrist instead of a gold pinky ring you break the "bling" monotony. But the key point is that whatever you do differently you do because you *feel* like doing it, not just to be different. If you are simply trying to force a break in sameness…

You are no different than the herd!

Moreover, the persona difference isn't only in your appearance. It is in your energy. Truth has a unique energy signature. People can pick up on it unconsciously. This is why we are drawn to some people we've just met even though they're not like us and yet also repelled by others that are apparently cut from exactly the same cloth as us. Because one was being genuine when they met us and the other was acting.

Remember that people buy based on feelings. When people first meet you they are "buying" the idea of spending more time with you. If they don't *feel* right about you they won't *buy* into spending more time with you.

So simply express yourself honestly and folks will be far more likely to engage more with you because they can feel you're being authentic, which automatically lowers their defenses and allows you to really get to know them.

Of course there are more elements that make up your Unique Sales Persona. Let's look at some more.

☑ DO... Create a UST – Unique Sales Title

The first phase of sales is like a boxing match. When you first meet someone, be it on the phone or at a networking event, they will ask you what you do. Though this may seem like a perfunctory and meaningless moment it is actually a pivotal point in your process with them.

If you say "I'm an accountant", the box for accountants in their brain opens up and you are dumped into it. The same holds true for "I sell IT services", "I'm an account manager with Mega-Big Manufacturing Corp", etc.

Their brain is looking to "match" you to a box, so it can file you away.

Their brain wants to **understand** you. The problem is that you automatically get generalized in their mind and it is very hard to get out of that box once you are in it!

As one of my GURUS Mentors, a master of *NLP*, taught me, "The brain sorts for difference." You can take advantage of this by forcing the buyer to create a new brain-box just for you.

The way to do this is by creating a UST – Unique Sales Title.

Example: One of my clients is a human resources consultant. But if you say "Human Resources Consultant" to prospects they automatically think they know what you do and stop listening.

Even if you state your specialization within HR consulting – such as "compensation planning" – prospects still assume they know what you do and stop listening.

We needed a way to get her prospects to listen beyond the first three seconds and make her more intriguing.

After a brainstorming session she finally blurted out that what she does is like "Cortez burning the ships." She leads people into the "jungle" of new business and away from the comfort of what they used to know.

Her new UST: I'm a ship burner!

The standard response to her new UST is, "What's that?"

At this point she can launch into talking about Cortez and burning the ships and draw parallels about what she does and the benefit of it. She has the prospect's attention and interest.

The UST has done its job. She has "out-boxed" her prospect!

☑ DO... Create a UCP - Unique Contrarian Position

Those of us who reside in the United States get to enjoy the wonders of a two-party system of government. That means that there are Republicans and Democrats. And depending upon which side you align with, your opinion is, "There is us and then there are those idiots."

Basically, as soon as you state which party you side with you are automatically alienating people from the other party. Yet most people actually hide or muddle their party affiliation. They say things like, "I'm a registered Democrat but I tend to vote Republican" or, "I vote for the best qualified candidate."

So, what we have is a lot of people who have taken a stand but just don't want anyone else to know what it is for fear of losing social equity.

Of course, as my GURUS mentors would tell you, alienation is a prerequisite to becoming a salebrity. Basically...

If everyone likes you no one will buy from you.

The truth is that you have to be controversial if you want high end buyers to pay attention to you and ultimately buy from you. Now, I'm not saying that you should create fake controversy to draw attention. That would not be genuine.

The way you become controversial is to simply use one of your inalienable rights...the freedom of speech. You have the right to state your opinions and feelings about anything you choose.

Now, when you openly and honestly state your feelings and opinions about what you sell and why you sell it, some people will not like your message and will move away from you. Good! Let them go. That's what you want.

Why? Because everyone who sticks with you will be that much more devoted to you. When you express yourself freely you've taken on the energy of a leader.

People follow leaders.

You will have people who follow you, become your clients and buy...and buy more...because of your leadership capacity. This is the ultimate point of becoming a salebrity.

You not only want to have people who love you...but also people who hate you.

If you doubt this, then I suggest you check out *Private Parts*, the story of radio shock jock Howard Stern's rise to stardom. There is a section in the book (and film version) where they show that people who loved Stern listened to him for 1.5 hours. But the people who hated him listened for 2.5 hours! And both groups listened to him for exactly the same reason..."I want to see what he'll say next."

Using this strategy Howard Stern went from being an unknown disc jockey in tiny markets to ruling the New York City airwaves to being paid half a billion dollars to move over to satellite radio. So, I'm pretty sure it will work for you.

Of course, if you know Howard Stern's work, you know he is anything but your typical disc jockey or talk radio guy. He has crafted a real-life characterization of himself that brings out his unique persona. His long hair, big nose, deep voice, childlike chuckle and sunglasses have become trademarks that cannot be mistaken.

More importantly, though, his UCP has catapulted him and his sales into the stratosphere…literally!

☑ DO… Create a USA – Unique Sales Avatar

In the last few years the word "avatar" has become very popular. First there was a cartoon with that name. Then more and more websites asked members to create avatars for themselves and finally James Cameron's blockbuster movie cemented the word into the general psyche.

Most of these versions of "avatar" revolve around having something outside of yourself that you can manipulate, such as an image or machine.

However, one of my mentors has taken "avatar" to a whole new level. She believes in creating Sales Avatars. But rather than this avatar being something outside of you, you are inside it. In other words…

Your Sales Avatar is you.

You might ask why you need a Sales Avatar when you are quite capable of going and doing sales as you are. That may be true, but most people do not bring the full power of their individual being to sales situations because they are constantly concerned with what the customer thinks of them. This puts them in the position of constantly second- guessing themselves and losing control of who they are in the moment.

When you create a Sales Avatar you come into each sales situation already complete and being the version of yourself you wish to maintain throughout the process. You no longer have to focus on yourself and can be assured that you are being who and how you wish to be.

Basically, creating a Sales Avatar means consciously choosing ahead of time the version of yourself you wish to bring to sales situations, instead of the version your unconscious might throw together as you are busy talking to clients.

This is a subtle but incredibly powerful distinction.

And, in case you think this runs counter to "being genuine", the exact opposite is true. You are more genuine than ever. This is because you have decided who you want to be and what standard you want to live up to in every sales situation when you are away from clients and pressure.

You create your Avatar in your genuine space, and therefore it is your genuine self, without all the mind junk that barrages you when you are speaking to clients.

How-To: Create Your Unique Sales Avatar

(HINT: Imagine you are creating an action figure of yourself that you have to live in.)

1. Select three words that describe what you stand for when doing sales with customers (for example, trust, contribution and fun). These words will guide the rest of the steps.

2. Make a list of three people you admire, in business or outside of business, that also embody or exemplify the three words you selected.

3. Watch videos of them speaking and/or read books they have written or speeches they have delivered. Then mimic their presentations or read their words as you believe they would read them. Do this aloud until you feel you are capturing their energy in the way you say it.

4. Examine their dress and tools. Dress like them, but only so far as it feels comfortable to you and is acceptable in your field. Copy some of the tools they use, such as a phone, watch, pen, glasses, etc. that they might have used for dramatic effect during a speech, like jabbing the air with a pen. Use tools that fit with you and that you feel comfortable using.

5. Once you have locked in steps one through four and have your avatar, select a phrase that describes who you are energetically now, such as "edgy communicator" or "kooky genius analyzer" or "enlightened leader." This will be the phrase you can say to yourself

each time you are going to speak with clients to remind you of your avatar self.

Make sure to regularly practice and reinforce your avatar aspects. As you live them over and over again you will find that they become you and vice versa.

Now, go make James Cameron proud!

☑ DO... Create a UTP – Unique Technology Position

Many of the high end salespeople I work with love to tell me all about their decades of experience. They throw this out there in an attempt to keep their pride when they first sit down with me. They need my help; they just don't want to admit it!

Rather than trying to overcome their pride, I feed it! After all, they have been working hard, if not effectively, for a long time. They have a lot of experience and they have a way of doing things that is unique to them. It's also the thing that can multiply their income in no time!

One of my GURUS Mentors, an expert in copywriting, once walked me through the art of writing bestselling business books...because he is also a ghost writer!

He explained that it didn't matter how much great information you put into a business book. If the readers couldn't organize it in their heads, they'd just forget and not use it. That meant that no one would recommend the book and...it would die a quick death in the bargain bin.

He said that the best books, the ones that the authors could build entire companies on, had a system or process or steps, like Covey's *Seven Habits*, Blanchard's *One Minute Manager* tactics, Rackham's *SPIN Selling*...or even my *GURUS Selling System*.

Having a process that readers could read, engage and use made the book have more meaning for them. Therefore, they were more likely to read the book and recommend it to others, which is…

The secret to a best seller!

You can use the same concept in your sales process. Create your own technology!

Example: Another of my GURUS Mentors was a top salesperson in the IT realm from the late 1990's to early 2000's. He was a run-of-the-mill salesperson until he decided to create his Unique Technology Position.

He would meet with a client and rather than start talking about what he sold, and before launching into a bunch of questions, he would introduce them to his process called IDOL.

IDOL stood for:

- Identify if the client really has any problems to be addressed
- Define one problem that the client wants to solve now
- Offer only what the client actually needs – no more, no less
- Let the client choose what is best for the client

When he explained that he had a unique technology that he put himself and his clients through in order to best serve the client, he automatically stood head and shoulders above every other salesperson who came in just going through the motions.

Now, honestly, every other salesperson may have had the exact same way of handling the sales process. The difference is that they did not *name* it and share it with the client!

My mentor was special simply because he was the only guy with his own technology!

Creating your own UTP is relatively simple.

How-To: Create your Unique Technology Position

1. Choose an aspect of your sales process. It could be the entire process. Or it could be just a piece of the process, such as an analysis of needs, inventory breakdown, initial meeting process, etc.

2. Break the process into steps. Try to keep the number of steps low, say no more than 7 and no less than 3.

3. Give the process a name. It can be "Steps" or "Habits" or "Levels" or "Waves", like Covey's Seven Habits. Or you can create an acronym for it like GURUS Selling.

That's it. You've got your own UTP!

Now, introduce it to all your new prospects when you first connect with them, and watch your credibility increase immediately.

☑ DO... Create a UMN – Unique Meeting Name

Do you like to set up "meetings" with clients? Of course you do. It only makes sense. After all, how can you get to know a client and learn about their needs if you don't meet with them?

The problem is that the client has been asked to have meetings with everybody who wants to sell them something. Therefore, meetings have become boring for the client. Also, the client automatically puts their guard up since they know that the other party at the meeting is looking to make a sell.

One of my GURUS mentors taught me a supremely simple and elegant twist that puts this whole issue to bed.

She told me to stop having "sales meetings."

Instead of sales meetings, my mentor told me to give the meeting a title and a beneficial outcome.

Example: When I was starting out as a business coach I used to try and set up meetings with prospects. This met with mediocre results.

After working with my mentor, I renamed my meetings and called them *Profit Jumpstart Sessions*. I also promised the client that I would give them at least one strategy during the session that could help them generate a 20% increase in sales in three months or less. And I was always true to my offer.

My conversion rate tripled within one month!

All because I changed what I called the meeting and gave a little benefit.

Did I change what I said or did? No. The meeting was still the same. I simply *positioned* the meeting to have more value than just a "meeting." When people value something, they are more interested, more engaged and more likely to take action.

SECTION THREE

How do <u>GURUS</u> convert more leads into clients?

Chapter 7
<u>BE</u> Aligned

"Just as your car runs more smoothly and requires less energy to go faster and farther when the wheels are in perfect alignment, you perform better when your thoughts, feelings, emotions, goals, and values are in balance."
— Brian Tracy

Imagine if you were in an airport and as you stood in the terminal you looked out at the plane you were about to board and noticed that the wings didn't line up. You'd quickly run over to the counter and tell them about the problem.

Now, what if the person behind the counter said they knew about the problem and, since all the pieces of the plane were there and connected, they were willing to risk your life and fly the plane anyway. Would you get on board? Hell, no! And you'd never fly that airline again!

Yet every day, millions of salespeople risk their livelihoods by getting "on board" sales processes with prospects that are out of alignment. They bring all the pieces of the sales process together and figure, just like the flight assistant, that if all the pieces are there that is good enough. And then...

They wonder why they crash and burn!

Alignment is so vital and necessary in every aspect of life that I am amazed at how many salespeople ignore it.

In sales, *alignment* means being truly aligned with your client. This doesn't mean just "understanding their problem" or "knowing what they are talking about."

Alignment with a client is like that kinship and synchronicity you have with your best friend. You can finish each other's sentences because it's like you almost have the same mind. It is scary and funny at the same time.

You trust your best friend because you know, without having to ask, that they instinctively know what is best for you because it is also what is best for them. No fear. No checking. Just trust and confidence.

This is the level that salespeople want to get to...in theory. In action, however, most salespeople are so focused on trying to make a deal that they lose the opportunity to make a friend who then becomes a client... long term.

☑ DO... Follow the MAP

"No one has ever achieved extraordinary results through ordinary efforts." – Erik Luhrs

Like anything worth doing, aligning does take some time. How long it takes varies depending upon how closely two people are or are not aligned initially. There are also other factors, unique to each individual, that can slow down or speed up the process.

Of course, alignment begins with you, during your time of becoming genuine and also creating your Unique Sales Persona. This would be your IA or "Individual Alignment."

Once you wish to align with another person you are moving into the MAP or Mutual Alignment Process.

There are four phases of the MAP that lead us from starting with a prospect all the way to securing the pact (deal).

We will explore them in depth as we go on. To start, however, here they are with brief descriptions.

I. The PAIN and PROBLEM illusion

This is the beginning of our time with the prospect. We build rapport, empathize with their pain, realize their true problem and, ultimately, get to their UBP or Unique Buying Position.

II. Discovering Limitless POTENTIAL

This is the part of the process where we help the client see that there is a solution to their problem and an end to their pain, with far greater outcomes than they may yet have imagined.

III. Forging the ALLIANCE

This is the portion of the process within which we become the ally of the client as well as the portal for them to achieve their desired outcomes.

IV. The Perfunctory PROPOSAL

This is just the part where the formal paperwork gets done.

☑ DO... Dispel the Pain and Problem Illusion

"You don't have any problems. You only think you do."
– Dr. Wayne Dyer

Did you ever notice that sometimes salespeople talk about the need to discover and solve the client's pain, while other salespeople say they need to discover and solve their client's problem? Well, the funny thing is that they are both right and both wrong.

Let's look first at **problems**. The world "problem" is a label. If I go outside and it's a bright sunny summer day, the day is great. If however, I have skin cancer, the sun is now a "problem." This same model is true for every "problem" under the sun.

Problems are subjective

Problems are based **around** situations. They are logistical in nature. They are the convergence of two or more factors that produce results that the client wishes were different. That's it.

A situation "I don't like" is a problem

Now, a problem can be miniscule, like an untied shoelace, or monstrous, like the failure of the levies in New Orleans during Hurricane Katrina. But it is always something logistical and tangible.

Therefore, "problems" really only exist in the mind.

Let's talk about "pain."

Real "pain" is a physiological response to a stimulus that is unpleasant, like cutting your finger or getting punched.

For our purposes, however…in the realm of sales…pain is an emotional response that is brought on by how people think *about* their problems, like feeling bad that your friend can't visit you this weekend because she has to work. The problem is her having to work. The "pain" is the loss of the joy you were expecting.

Pains can be small, like "a pain in the ass", or they can be huge, like "there is a hole in my life now that my father has died." But they are ultimately intangible and subjective in nature.

Therefore pain, like all other emotions, resides in the heart.

Pain can arise in the buyer because their desired outcomes are vague or incomplete.

Example: The client thinks they want $1MM in sales, but what they really want is their house and vacation house free and clear and $250K a year while working less or not at all. This internal disconnect between what someone thinks they want and what they really want leads to confusion and ultimately to pain.

When salespeople go in to meet with a client they will usually try to sell **to** or **at** the client's problem. The logic behind this is that salespeople can most easily see what the logistical problem is with a client. And in the rush to make an offer and get a deal, they will go for the obvious problem solution.

However, as my GURUS mentors taught me, we must get to **why** people want what they want, **what** exactly they want or need, and exactly how to deliver that to them.

The old logic says, "People buy based on emotion and justify later with logic." I disagree, and here is why.

There are three types of buying decisions!

They are: Logic-based, Heart-based, and Feeling-based.

Logic-based buying decisions are very common and very poor. When people are trying to make logical buying decision it automatically means a long sales process. This is because they are "weighing options" and trying to "get more for less."

These are the buying decisions that usually lead to one-time sales because the buyer is ultimately unexcited with their logical choice.

Emotion-based buying decisions are less common in high end sales, but are also poor. When people make emotional buying decisions it is because they are in a panic and need a "solution" now. They are choosing blindly.

Once the panic passes the buyer realizes that they've made an irrational decision and instantly feel buyer's remorse. These are the buying decisions that usually end with demands for returns and refunds or some other form of credit.

People make their best buying decisions based on FEELINGS, when their heart's emotions and mind's logic are balanced. So...

Feelings are NOT emotions!

They are the mid-ground between emotions and thoughts. You can FEEL emotions, like, "I feel sad", but you can also FEEL thoughts, like, "I feel this isn't going to work." The FEELING is the controlling mechanism in either case.

So, if logic lives in the mind and emotions live in the heart, then where do feelings live?

Feelings live in the gut...literally!

This is where the brain and heart meet.

Every human being has two nervous systems, not just one.

Although we normally talk about the central nervous system, the one that controls blinking, breathing walking, etc., there is also another nervous system at work; the enteric nervous system.

The enteric nervous system is housed in the tissue around the esophagus, stomach, small intestine and colon. It has neurons and neurotransmitters just like those in the brain. It is able to act independently. It can learn and remember. It creates "gut feelings."

So part of the gut acts like the brain, a purely non-mechanical organ. But the gut also acts like the heart, a mechanical organ. The gut is both a thinking and an acting system...the only one in your body.

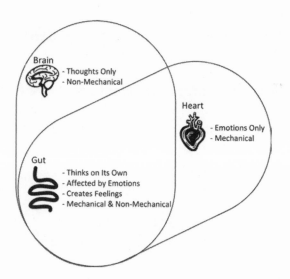

The Unique Buying Position resides in the gut. This is why when you have a true "aha moment" it is as if your mind temporarily empties and your heart does as well and you *feel* the truth of the "aha" in your core...your gut.

Imagine if your clients felt an "aha" that you helped inspire when dealing with you.

You'd have affected their core!

Do you think they'd have any choice but to buy from you?

There are no factoids or price cuts that counteract the truth that a human being holds within themselves. We will always fight for the truths we hold, no matter what.

If you don't believe me, look at how many millions of people have fought and died for their religions, their countries, their ethnicities.

History itself is a testament to the UBP!

☑ DO... Stop Making Sales Calls

The standard practice, if you do sales face to face or even via web conference, is to move a lead from the lead generation stage to the sales meeting or sales call stage as quickly as possible.

It is at this stage that most sales are lost.

As one of my GURUS mentors put it, "Excited by the prospect of an eventual sale, the typical salesperson looks to speed-date their way through rapport and get right on into the client's problem so they can angle their solution and pitch their wares."

Rapport is the doorway to alignment. It is not just a perfunctory activity you do before someone hands you a purchase order and a check.

Your concern, compassion, interest and patience in building rapport stand as a testament to what kind of person you are. Unconsciously the client picks this up from you. If you speed through rapport, they will think you are looking to "get lucky" rather than build a relationship. At this point your funnel has broken, and the client will fall out.

All of my GURUS mentors stressed the need to focus only on rapport at this point because it shows you're genuinely concerned about getting to know the other person as a person and then, only if there is a genuine possibility for business, will you explore that at a time that is natural for both of you.

Therefore, instead of thinking of your first meeting with a client as a 'sales call'…

It is more accurate to call it an Alignment Call.

This assures that you are thinking about alignment and not the sale.

☑ DO… Use the Three C's of the Alignment Call

Assumption can mean making an ass out of u and me. But it can also mean bypassing a buyer's resistance and strengthening your relationship. In this case, I am talking about *assuming* you are a not a salesperson.

You see, when you first meet a client they are waiting for the pitch. They know it is coming and they are looking for you to go straight into "data dump" mode. This would be when you tell them all the great and wonderful things your solution can do to start to set them up for the pitch to close the deal.

Of course, as one of my GURUS mentors told me, "The easiest way to get around a buyer's resistance is to avoid it altogether."

Clients don't want to listen. They want to speak.

They have an issue that vexes them and they want to understand it first and solve it second. Basically, they really want to talk out their problems.

This is why GURUS Salespeople actually play three parts in alignment calls…

I.   Consultant

II.   Coach

III.   Critic

Let's look at the Consultant first.

The Consultant comes out in the first phase of the alignment call. Salespeople want to sell stuff whereas Consultants want to solve problems. When you become a consultant you shift into their mindset. The consultant starts off by asking questions, lots of questions.

Now you might say that salespeople also ask questions, and they do. But it is the *intention* of the questions that is different. Salespeople tend to ask linear questions aimed at connecting a problem to *their* solution.

Consultants ask questions across all levels, from the 1,000-foot level all the way down to the minute detail level. They need to comprehend scope, scale and interconnectivity of factors before they can begin to figure out what the real problem is and how to solve it.

They thrive on puzzles rather than prizes.

The consultant is able to lay out all the factors and the interplay of the factors among levels for the client. The client can then fully grasp their problem and begin to see beyond it.

At this point the consultant can begin to offer a solution.

Now we move into the Coach phase.

Once the solution has been offered the client has to process what has been shown and offered to him internally.

This is where tangible reality mixes with intangible feelings. The client starts to filter and ultimately distort what they have learned based on their past experiences. Again, the client is trying to fit things into boxes in their head…even if the pieces don't fit well.

At this point the client is in jeopardy of believing whatever bullshit pops into their head and closing the door on the alignment process.

They are Mindf***ing themselves!

Even though they consciously want to solve their problem, their unconscious is having a party with their brain.

At this point they need a coach. They need someone who can help them to properly absorb, comprehend and use the data that has been given to them.

Now you are no longer solving puzzles. You are doing therapy. I know it sounds weird but it's true.

I regularly speak with VPs of sales and CEOs and even when I give them the most cut and dried solutions they will start to ask me the most off-the-wall questions. This is because their minds are trying to make sense of the solutions. But, since their mind has no previous reference points because there have been only problems up to now, they start to look for more problems...even if they have to create them.

You've seen this in your own life, when you've had a friend who was messing up and you gave them great advice and yet two weeks later they were still making the same mistakes.

As the coach you help the client through their internal issues. As a by-product, you will be deepening rapport and alignment - all of which creates a stronger bond between you two.

Last is the Critic.

Once the client finally comprehends what you have told them and they accept it correctly, they then need to *feel* confident that the solution you have presented works for them.

They need reassurance.

One of my GURUS mentors built a chain of jewelry stores before selling them for a hefty profit. She told me that when she first started out and was doing all her own sales, she was amazed how many women would come in to try on jewelry and then not buy even when they needed an item immediately, like for a fancy dinner the same evening.

At first my mentor just accepted this as part of doing business. But then she realized that many of the women seemed intimidated by the jewelry, as if it were *too* beautiful. She knew there was a little voice saying bad things in their heads.

So, she started to tell the clients how beautiful they themselves were and how the jewelry "brought that out" even more or how it "framed" their faces or how it was the "icing on the cake."

With just these kinds of polite reassurances here sales increased dramatically!

As a side note, all of these women had friends. They told their friends how wonderful my mentor was, so she got a ton of referral business simply by being a good critic.

☑ DO… Use the Fourth C Too

The Fourth C is separate from the first three because it is not a role you play but rather an energy you create.

As Jeffrey Gitomer says, "People hate to be sold, but they love to buy."

What Jeffrey is saying is that you should avoid "selling" people because they automatically feel it and resist it. Instead, you should create the compulsion to buy.

The secret is to compel rather than sell. So…

Compulsion is the fourth C

The compulsion to buy, and to buy enthusiastically, is born from the desire for instant gratification. So, rather than being a moth to the flame (chasing the sale), be the flame for the moth (have the sale chase you).

For years I have used an odd little story to make sure this idea *sticks* in the minds of my clients and students.

Imagine you are in a chair and you are unable to move your arms or legs. You are alone in a room that has only one door. Stuck, *lovingly*, into your right quadriceps is a four-inch Emerson Combat Knife. It hurts like hell and you are bleeding out badly!

The door opens and two men walk in. One man is short, slightly balding, wearing glasses and a doctor's coat. The other man looks like a bum off the street. He is chewing a toothpick and doesn't smell too good.

The doctor speaks first. "I'm a doctor who deals in pain management. I will evaluate your pain, analyze the causes of your pain and offer remedies. Over time we should be able to reduce your pain so that it is manageable. We may even be able to eliminate it if we..." He goes on like this for five minutes.

When the doctor is done you look at the other guy.

The bum spits out his toothpick and says, "I'm a knife puller. I pull knives out of things."

So, which guy would you hire?

As you can see, when the client fully comprehends their problem and the salesperson clearly defines the solution in terms of the problem, and the client seeks instant gratification, the sale is a given.

Now, that is not to say that you are looking for clients in agony. Of course, the clients who will love you the most and revere you the most are the ones who feel that you saved them from the greatest pain-problem. And the truth is that...

> ### *Everyone who connects with you has a problem and is in pain in some way.*

You do a great service by helping them to truly comprehend that pain-problem for what it is, so they are no longer living in an illusion that could hurt them even more down the line.

☑ DO... Relish Your Ignorance

One of the things that most sales managers, sales books and sales trainers will pound into your head is that you need to learn as much as possible about your prospect **before** meeting them, so research them and their company to the Nth degree.

The logic behind this is that the more you know about the person and company beforehand the more understanding you will have of them. And it is true that you will know more. But…it is also what can cost you the sale.

Several of my GURUS mentors stressed that learning as much as possible about someone and their company before you meet them creates an artificial sense of knowledge and understanding in you.

You may know things **about** the person but you don't really know the **person**. Nonetheless, armed with articles, stats and bios you believe that you do. This false sense of knowing automatically stifles the rapport building that is necessary to create trust and alignment.

When you already believe that you **know** something you will not ask about it or, if you do, you will ask but not really listen, believing that you already know the answer.

Also, when you ask about something you already know you are actually being false at that moment and therefore you have broken the alignment of your genuine self.

So, ignorance is the best policy!

You actually want to know as **little** as possible about the person.

Now, you might say that there are clients out there that are expecting you to do your "homework" and expect you to know volumes about them, and they will be thrown off if you don't. Good!

When you go in and give the client what they are expecting you are again reinforcing their belief that you are like every other salesperson they have spoken to. You are no longer different and no longer interesting!

Further, since people love to talk about themselves, when you ask honest, probing questions you are allowing them an opportunity to educate you on their favorite subject: Themselves!

Again, this puts the client at ease since they can sense that you are A) honestly interested and B) not faking it.

Voila! Yet another automatic defense goes down!

☑ DO... Act like a Prick

At the request of *Chief Executive* Magazine, I was asked to take part in a closed door meeting at the *New York Stock Exchange*. There were about a dozen of us in the room, including the chairman of *McDonalds*, the CEO of *McDonalds*, the chairman of *Xerox* and several other prominent CEOs and business leaders.

The topic of discussion was "How to restore trust in CEOs."

All of my colleagues made well-grounded and logical arguments. They mainly spoke about ways that CEOs could pay more attention to the needs of society and the community, and how they could display more leadership in public, etc. It was all very wise and highbrow stuff. And...

After about an hour I could NOT take it anymore!

I proceeded to go on a twelve-minute diatribe that was contrary to virtually everything they were saying. I basically said, "Who cares about looking good and getting nice PR?"

I pointed out that there were three types of people: Those who will buy your stuff, those who won't buy your stuff, and the media who will roast you or toast you so long as it sells more ad space.

First, I told them that they should ignore the media because the media doesn't care; they'll print what they want.

Then I said they should ignore the people who won't buy from them, because even if they could make those people believe they were nice those people still wouldn't spend money for their products or services, which means they'd waste millions of dollars on pointless PR campaigns.

Finally, I said they should only focus on and enhance their messaging with the folks who will buy their stuff, because that would produce more income. And then, if they still wanted to look good for the general public, they were free to donate all the extra money they made and saved to charities or other civic organizations.

When I stopped there was stunned silence for about ten seconds. I had made my point.

Afterwards the editor of the magazine shook my hand, gave me a knowing smile and said, "Sometimes it pays to be the contrarian." He would know. He has seen the best and the worst that the corporate world has to offer.

I had made my point, and a deep impact, because I had acted like a prick.

Now, I don't mean "prick" in the slang sense of male genitalia. I mean **prick** as something that pierces or cuts. I had **cut** open the cocoon of formal theoretical hyperbole (AKA fancy words and a bunch of bullshit) that had been going on in the room.

Of course, the same thing happens tens of thousands of times a day in the world of high end sales.

CXO's surrounded by yes-men who dress, walk and talk like them meet with salespeople who dress, walk and talk like them. And they discuss problems in theoretical ways and polite tones. Then there is the polite pitch, the polite request for a proposal, followed by the polite kiss-off. It's all very polite.

And the CXO thinks that is what they want: Polite – Polite - Polite. Of course this doesn't get to the heart of their problem or pain. It's just more exercises in futility in the cocoon of polite sameness.

My GURUS mentors who engage in C-level sales realize that cocoons won't burst themselves. So, if the caterpillar of a problem is ever going to become the butterfly of a solution...

Someone has to prick open that cocoon!

Now, to be a good prick you have to be willing to be a little gruff, straightforward and controversial. You must throw punches instead of pulling them. It has to hurt when you get pricked. If it doesn't hurt, then you weren't pricked. And *almost* pricked won't burst any cocoons.

At first the client may be thrown off or even feel offended by you cutting through the normal crap and telling it like it is. And that is good! They need to be shaken before they can recover.

You might worry about bruising their egos. Don't! Remember that they *want* you to solve their problems, because if you don't then they will suffer far more ego-bashing and career destruction than your momentary pricking could ever do.

Now your job is to validate your statements and give the client a new perspective on their situation. The more simplistic you can make their situation seem, the more they will respect you, because the situation has been overwhelming them up to that point. And since respect is a cornerstone of trust and rapport, you're pricking is also working for you.

I will be honest and tell you that being confrontational with clients is not for the faint of heart. But remember that your mission when meeting with a client is not to *sell* them, but to *help* them. If you skirt the truth in order to be respectable and polite you are only allowing them to remain trapped by their situation and you have moved no closer to making a sale.

☑ DO… Call Your Shot

"Under-promise and over-deliver!" This is a battle cry used by millions of salespeople throughout the world.

Of course, the downside is that when you do under-promise, or just don't promise anything at all, there is nothing for you to live up to. This causes many salespeople to be lazy or fail to *wow* clients simply because the client had no basis or benchmark to measure what was delivered.

Therefore, even when salespeople do deliver some value it is hard for the client to know because they assume it was just part of their regular process.

No pizzazz. No wow.

Though baseball has many legendary players, none is more iconic than Babe Ruth. And he sealed his legendary status in 1932 when he famously called his shot in the third game of the World Series.

Taunting the Chicago Cubs, he defiantly pointed to center field as he stepped up to the plate. He did what no other player had ever dared to do: He called his shot! And shortly thereafter he made good on his promise and smacked a curve ball into the center field bleachers for a home run.

Many of my GURUS mentors gladly call their shots, especially during alignment meetings. And even though the gestures may not be as big, bold and ballsy as Ruth's on the plate, they carry great weight with the client.

Now, calling your shot isn't complicated. You need only say something as simple as, "today I will break down the situations that are causing your current issues. I will then outline the options you have, given your resources and timeline. And then we will decide on the best course of action for you."

In truth you are simply pre-framing the outcome of the meeting. It was going to happen anyway, but now the client feels anticipation instead of being unsure what is going on or what is going to happen.

GURUS TWEAK: As you may have noticed the last sentence of my imaginary shot call was, "And then we will decide on the best course of action for you."

Now, obviously you can't actually control if or when the client will decide. But when you openly pull **them** into **your** plan, and make good on doing all the things you promised and can control, the client will feel a desire to help you complete what you've set out to do. Therefore, in this case, he'd be highly prone to making a decision that day when you're done, instead of putting it off.

CHAPTER 8
<u>BE</u> WITH IT

After I do a speech or presentation for any large group, the thing most folks ask me about is the UBP – Unique Buying Position. They hear the words, feel the concept and want to understand it, so they can act upon it.

The truth is that getting to, working with and leveraging the UBP is as much art as it is science.

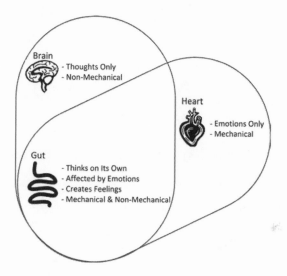

As you know, the UBP resides in the gut. It is the meeting point of the heart and mind. That is why it is both rational and irrational, cautious and yearning. It is fluid in nature because it flows inside of the client. It slides back and forth between problem and pain instantly. The right or wrong words can win it or lose it quickly.

In his book *Blink*, Malcolm Gladwell lays out the hows and whys of people's decision making, and it all points to one conclusion: People's thoughts and feelings solidify in just a moment. ...

People's feelings solidify in just a moment.

The UBP works that quickly too. So getting to a skill level where you can work with the UBP will take time. But trust, as I did, in the GURUS and you will master it.

Since we essentially covered the processes to get **to** the UBP in the last chapter, in this chapter we'll explore the methodologies for working **with** the UBP.

☑ DO... Beware of "Why"

One of the methodologies I use in working with clients is field observation. I will sit in on their sales calls, lead generation calls or conference calls to see what they do and how they do it.

And there is one word that salespeople throw around so callously and destructively that it often makes me physically wince when I hear them say it. That word is "why."

Now, you may ask, "Why don't you like 'why'?"(a question that would not make me wince, by the way.)

Let's dissect "why" and see what the problem is.

Most folks see "why" as just a word to begin a question: "Why did you lie?" "Why did he call?" "Why weren't the tickets there?" etc.

However...

"Why" is a doorway to creation for the opportunistic mind.

It allows for total imagination, subjectivity and ambiguity in an answer. "Why" exists in the realm of the intangible.

Example: If you ask a client, "Why did you choose not to buy from us?" they can say something simple like, "Your prices are more than we can afford." Or they can just run on: "You're too expensive, and I didn't feel secure in your track record, and we're not able to handle the schedule we knew would come from working with you, and…"

At this point the client is irrationally justifying and solidifying their reasons for not buying from you. Their imagination is convincing them again and again that they should not buy from you. After just thirty seconds of this, your chances of ever getting back in with them are slim to none.

And it's not even that they are correct in their reasoning. But they are correct in **their** mind, over and over, and **that** is what matters to them.

However, if you simply use another word, such as "what", things change dramatically.

Example: "What made you choose not to buy from us?" "What" dictates and enables tangible thoughts. The responses will be more grounded, like, "We couldn't afford the fee" or "It was part price and part speed. The other vendor could deliver faster." "What" narrows the focus, especially if you empower it with "specifically" (i.e. "What specifically…?")

Of course, there is a good side to why when it is used at the right time in the right way.

If you are meeting a prospect and you want to solidify them into being more secure about you, you can ask, "Why do you know we can help you?"

At this point their imagination will search for and make up reasons. And it will again solidify and reinforce their position, which now is to work **with** you.

After a minute of convincing themselves of your or your products' worth, it will be hard for them not to buy from you.

☑ DO… Smile Through the Client's Pain

Though it may seem hard to believe, people will thank you, and buy from you, if you make them feel pain…the right way.

As one of my GURUS mentors put it…

> *"Until there is pain, there can be no pleasure."*

As you help people get down to their deeper pain, what we call a level 10 pain, it can be a test of your will. As they become more annoyed, upset, irritated, etc. with your questions and direction, it can be very attractive to just back down and be the polite salesperson again.

Of course, as all of my GURUS mentors would tell you, even though the clients may not like this part of the sale process, you are truly helping them. Arguably you are helping them more than anyone else, because they themselves have no idea what their level 10 pain is or that it even exists.

You are helping them gain clarity, which everyone needs before they can begin to fix things. Also, as people clarify their pain, the answer will often become self-evident and simple, so you don't have to have be Einstein to help them figure out solutions. Just by helping and connecting, usually you will get a new customer.

And even if your product or service is ultimately not the solution for them, you will gain tremendous credibility with them, which can translate into referrals or more sales opportunities down the line.

☑ DO... Find the Pain – Problem Point

As I have alluded to before, there is a distinct difference between a client's personal pain and the logistical problem that triggers that pain. In order to maintain flow in the sales process you must break down the client's thoughts where they tangle pain and problem together as one entity.

Again, this is the doorway to the UBP.

How-To: Untangle the Pain - Problem Point

1. Remember that "people's biggest problem is they don't know what their biggest problem is." By that logic, it is safe to say that the thing that causes people the most pain is *not* knowing exactly what hurts or exactly what is causing it.

   So, it is your job to stay as objective as possible and to keep your *1,000-foot view* on the situation. This means that no matter what they *say* is their pain or problem, you must take it with a grain (or ten) of salt, because they are stuck in the middle of their situation and their view is 100% subjective, limited and confused.

As the old Yiddish saying goes, "To a codfish stuck in a bucket of horseradish the world is horseradish." You must remain outside the "bucket" or else you risk accepting their reality and believing their limited beliefs, at which point you are as helpless as they are.

2. After you have the proper mindset, you must then help the client to break down their issues. This means that you capture and dismantle all complex concepts and questions.

Example: If a client says, "Our staff can't handle the required workload to meet the demand," you would have to seize on the concept and break it down by asking questions like...

- Which staff?
- Are you talking about all of the staff?
- What specifically can't they handle?
- What is the "required" workload?

Any of these kinds of questions will force the client to look at smaller pieces of their issue. As you get to smaller and smaller pieces, the problems and pains will begin to separate themselves. At this point solutions will become easier and more apparent.

3. Get the client to describe a tangible problem or to agree with you when you pinpoint it. Like I said, after you have broken things down into small pieces the problems and solutions should become self-evident.

Of course, what "should" happen and what does happen are often different. So, when you see a real lynchpin problem, and the client hasn't grasped that it *is* the lynchpin problem, you must call it out.

Example: Let's say you have been called in to help with a turnover problem. You see that the problem causing high turnover is the lack of steady leadership of teams, which in turn is caused by the boss firing managers on a regular basis, which in turn is caused by the boss never having set down actual expectations from the managers. Then you must tell the client, "It's the lack of set expectations that is causing your turnover problem."

4. Finally, your job is to get them to accept and agree with this tangible and correctable problem.

CAVEAT: Be careful that the client doesn't just *say* "yes" without really believing your version of the problem. You have to work with the client until they *own* that truth.

At this point you have the client's level 10 pain with, but separate from, their lynchpin problem, so you now have the situation that needs to be solved.

Another way to describe this is what I call the Problem – Cause Identification Process for Simplifying Sales.

As you can see from the diagram, disconnect happens in the mind of the buyer when you try to sell to a "symptom" (AKA shallow-level problem).

This is why clients don't buy
even when it is "logical."

They need to *feel* the solution, which only happens when you both agree on the cause (i.e. the level 10 problem).

At this point the client conceptualizes and feels the problem while simultaneously perceiving the pain. Now they can see that both come from one common source – the situation that needs to be resolved.

CHAPTER 9
<u>BE</u> ENGAGING

Once the client begins to see things differently there is a risk that they will fall into the "let me ponder that" syndrome. This is brought on by a situation that shows you that what you thought was "real" isn't. The buyer's mind wants to shut its doors for a while and make sense of this new perspective.

Of course, by shutting the doors…

Their mind is also shutting out you and the solution!

So, it is vitally important that you become highly engaging at this point. You must keep the buyer's attention on you and the outcome. After all, pondering solves nothing! And your responsibility, above all else, is to serve the client.

Let's look at the ways you can increase engagement and decrease your client's Attention Deficit Disorder.

☑ DO… Presentations without Doing Presentations

PRESENT - (adjective) Now being considered; actually here or involved: the present subject.

(verb) To offer for observation, examination, or consideration; show or display.

As you can see, "present" is both an adjective and a verb. So in a way it is static and in another way it is dynamic. And of course, anything static kills rapport.

The funny thing is that even though a verb is an <u>action</u> word….

The verb form of "Present" is actually the static version!

You may think I mistyped that last sentence, but I assure you I did not.

You see, when you do a presentation you are basically putting something out there and talking *about* it. It could be a car on display at an auto show, or a software package you are presenting to a CIO, or a consulting project you are presenting to a board, etc.

In all these instances something has been put on display (car, software, project idea) and is being talked *about* by the salesperson. The client is mute and listening.

They have become static!

As one of my GURUS Mentors drilled into my head, "If the process of putting something on display and talking about it actually produced steady sales, you'd be buying everything you saw advertised on TV last night…and you'd be broke by day's end."

Effective communication is a dynamic, two-way experience, which is hijacked for the duration of any sales presentation. So the adjective "present" (actually here or involved) ends up being the *dynamic* definition. This basically means that…

PowerPoint is pointless!

To make matters worse, most high end salespeople live and die by their pre-scripted presentations supported by…PowerPoint slides!

This truly puts the nail in the coffin of the presentation. Here's why…

First, it is the basic instinct of humans to assimilate as much information as they can in a situation so they can feel as if they know what is going on and, even more so, what is going to happen.

When a PP slide goes up, the first thing people do is read it. As soon as that happens they stop listening to the salesperson because they believe they already know what's coming.

They will then zone out until the next slide!

Of course this gives them more time to check their e-mail on their *BlackBerry*. Another victory for multi-tasking! Too bad it will cost you the sale.

Second, because so much information is being pushed on them so quickly, they aren't really *ingesting* it.

Imagine every sentence the salesperson says is an apple. It takes time to bite, chew, swallow and digest an apple. Now imagine dumping a whole apple orchard on someone and expecting them to be able to eat it in half an hour. Its sounds ridiculous…and that's because it is!

Third, the client is sitting in a darkened room with a salesperson assaulting their mind with intermittent visual stimulus and an overabundance of auditory information that overwhelms them from the get-go, while they are expected to sit quietly and watch.

These are the perfect settings for creating a trance or hypnotic state. So, don't be surprised if you see the client's eyes drooping. They are merely responding to the context and stimulus being given to them.

So, if you want to do an effective presentation, understand that…

It is not "your" presentation.
It is "our" communication.

So, how do we do that? How do we turn a static presentation into a dynamic communication that helps us align even more deeply with the client…?

☑ DO… Show the Client Your POWER

Obviously when you are going in to do a sales presentation you desire to communicate a certain amount of information to the client.

But rather than designing a complete forty-five-minute, front-to-back presentation (including jokes), you would be better served by going in less rehearsed and more honest. The reason is that honest intention and honest communication can't be achieved by pre-scripted means.

Several of my GURUS mentors have methodologies to bypass formal presentations. I've synthesized them into the POWER approach.

How-To: Take the POWER Approach

1. P - Prepare Bullet Points. Just like your pre-scripted presentation, you have certain material you want to cover. Simplify each point to its basest essence and write it down.

    This is actually easy. Just take whatever slides you were going to use and ask yourself, "What is the point I am trying to make with this slide?"

    Make sure that you only have one point per ten minutes of allotted time. So, if you have forty-five minutes for your presentation, you should have four or five bullet points to address.

    Don't worry. Once you get into a real discussion with the client, four or five main points will fill the time easily.

2. O - Open with a Bang. Walk in and make a statement that takes the clients off guard in an ultimately positive way.

    Example: If the client is waiting for you to talk about the value of your company's facility management services and you open by saying, "To be honest with you, your current facilities management provider is doing a great job. Wouldn't you agree?" You now have the client's full attention and their pattern...waiting for a one-sided presentation...has been completely interrupted.

    Now, obviously, you are going to show them the real value of hiring your company, because that kind of opening is a set-up. You know that your company is more cost efficient, faster, has more resources and will be more proactive. But by opening in a contrary way you throw them off.

    There are many, many different ways to open with a bang. This is just one example.

BE DO SALE

3. **W - Wait on the Presentation and Redirect.** This piece is the key! Remember that you DO NOT want to engage in a formal presentation at any time!

   Now, tell the client something like this: "I know we wanted to discuss widget warehousing in the presentation, but before I begin, I wanted to talk a little more about your widget material supply needs."

   At this point, use your first bullet point as the foundation of a question for the client, like "What is your cost per widget when you buy in metric tons?" They will, of course, answer.

   You have successfully put the presentation on indefinite hold!

4. **E - Engage in a Mastermind.** The client is now in a full-bore dynamic communication with you. Simply cover all the bullet points you've created, in the guise of give-and-take questions and conversations.

   This dynamic communication allows you and the client to align faster and more easily than any one-sided presentation.

   In case you are wondering, "When I do I get to show the client all our features and benefits?" The answer is: As needed.

   As you are uncovering the pains, problems, issues, logistical requirements, etc., you will be able to bring up and explain the applicable pieces of your solution. If you cover all the client's needs and there are still certain features of your solution that didn't come up, then guess what? They weren't needed! You just saved yourself from boring the client with stuff they didn't need to hear!

5. **R - Restate Everything as You Understand it and Get Agreement.** As the conversation progresses, take notes. At the end, review each of your bullet points and the subsequent questions/issues/objections the client raised about each one. Get agreement from the client that your observations were correct.

The client now feels better represented and understood, which equals deeper rapport and alignment. This keeps the momentum in the alignment process and drives you more quickly to the sale.

☑ DO... Talk Like a Human

Pre-scripted presentations tend to be recited robotically by salespeople, especially after they have done them a few dozen times. This is based on the mistaken belief that people's words are more important than the *way* those words are said.

As one of my GURUS mentors would tell you, if you have deep rapport and the best intentions…

"You can basically bark and create a sale with a client."

Now, obviously, I don't go around barking at clients. But the truth is that the manner in which words are *said* is far more important and engaging than the actual words that are said.

Human beings naturally speak in three different tones. They are question, statement and command. This is a reflection of how the mind works as it takes in, processes and responds to information.

I don't mean that people use the sentence structures of questions, statements and commands (even though they do). What I am saying is that they use the VOCAL QUALITIES of question, statement and command.

To prove it, simply go and call any of your friends or family members right now and engage in a three-minute conversation. Listen to how they talk. You will notice their tone of voice naturally flowing from questions to statements to commands: "Did you call your sister?" "I'm looking forward to spring." "Send me back that book I lent you!"

When you engage your clients you need to avoid the never-ending statement tone that comes from reciting pre-scripted presentations.

Also, remember that salespeople will often use statement *tonality* even when asking a pre-scripted question or giving a pre-scripted command.

This is because they are still reciting from their memory rather than having a dynamic conversation.

So when you let go of scripts, trust yourself and engage in dynamic conversation, this issue will simply take care of itself.

☑ DO... Set Tangible Outcomes

Now that you have thoroughly untangled the client's tangible problems from the associated pains, you need to set outcomes with the client.

The single biggest issue that plagues most sales is the lack of *tangible* problems (which we have already handled) and the lack of *tangible* outcomes (which we will address now).

Many clients will say things like, "I want more sales" or "We need more storage space" or "We need to save more money." Of course, one more sale for the year would be "more sales." One more foot of space would be "more storage space." And one cent less spent each year would be "more savings."

Obviously, none of these miniscule outcomes are what the client really wants. But since....

They set vague outcomes they got vague results!

For an outcome to be tangible and truly achievable it must have five elements...

I.   It must be specific and positive.

II. It must have the difference between now and then defined.

III. It must be something that can be controlled by the client and you.

IV. It must be rationally achievable even if grand in scope.

V.   It must be free of by-product resistance.

How-To: Create Tangible Outcomes for Clients

1. Specific and positive. The outcome must be stated in such a way that it is not open to interpretation and it must state what is desired as opposed to what isn't desired.

    "I want less turnover of employees and I don't want to hire any more whiners" is not a tangible outcome. "I want to reduce our turnover to at least equal or below our competitors' rates and I only want to hire folks with an MBA" is tangible.

    Now, you might say that "...turnover to at least equal or below our competitors' rates..." is not specific. You might then say that a target number like "ten percent or less in six months" is specific, and it is. However, there is no way of knowing if ten percent or less can be achieved in six months, if at all. So be wary of setting too specific and stringent outcomes.

2. Difference between now and then defined. The client and you must be keenly aware of the current situation, the desired outcome and <u>all</u> the things that will have to change for one situation to become the other.

    This is the <u>only</u> way that the client and you will be able to comprehend the scope of change that has to be committed to.

    Many times clients will say no to you because they hear the outcome but they can't **comprehend** it. This creates unconscious confusion, which leads to a no.

3. Something that can be controlled by the client and you. The client, or you on behalf of the client, must be able to fully perform and maintain the necessary actions to achieve the outcome.

    Saying that you want to "close 100% more deals this year" is not something you can control. Saying that you "will go from making five hours of lead generation calls a week to ten hours" is something you can control.

The lack of control is another factor that can create confusion and disbelief in clients.

4. Rationally achievable even if grand in scope. It's okay to dream big, as long as you have a plan that is within the realm of possibility.

   If you go in to a client and tell them that your IT solution will increase their revenues by 200% in one year, but your plan involves a lot more ifs than thens, that shows that your goal is more irrational exuberance than rational planning.

   When you can go in and say that your IT solution will increase revenues by 200% and you can show a step-by-step plan, that is feasible, even if it requires everything going 100% correctly and full participation by everyone. It is rational even if grand in scope.

   And of course, any plans that require less dependence on 100% perfection are even more feasible.

   NOTE: Be sure to avoid making your plans so safe that they are under whelming. The idea of "under-promise and over-deliver" was valid twenty years ago. In today's market, clients want you to over-promise and double-over-deliver.

5. Free of by-product resistance. In the past you may have been in a situation where you offered a client everything they asked for, exactly as they wanted it, and even saved them more money than anyone else and they still said no.

   The reason this happens is that they have a resistance to the by-products of going after what they said they wanted.

   A simple example is weight loss. Many people commit to weight loss, begin to eat healthier diets and exercise and even like how they feel about themselves after a few days or weeks. Then they stop, pig out and give up.

   Why? Because they forgot about their fat friends who don't want to slim down. Their friends started to treat them differently. Every pound they lost seemed to drive a bigger wedge between them and their fat friends. So, the fear of losing their friends overcame their desire to lose weight. Boom! Diet dead!

High end buyers can have similar kinds of resistors in their world which they may or may not be aware of.

You must ferret out these resistors and inoculate against them for the good of your client.

At this point you will have a tangible outcome that meets the needs, hopes and desires of your client.

CHAPTER 10
<u>BE</u> INSPIRATIONAL

"Using no way as way.
Having no limitation as limitation." – Bruce Lee

Pink Floyd once said, "I have become comfortably numb." The same can be true of clients. Even though we have helped them to separate their problem from their pain and shown them a solution, it doesn't mean that they will jump up and say, "I'll take it!"

Many times the client has been dealing with the issue so long that they have become oddly accustomed to it. And, like an abused spouse, they may not be ready to part with the issue even though they know what it is. Yes, this sounds absurd, even unbelievable, and yet it's true.

One of my GURUS mentors told me a story that exemplifies this.

My mentor was a salesman at a BMW dealership. One of his clients referred a friend to him.

The man came into the dealership, test drove several cars, and liked one particular model. They talked about terms, pricing and interest rates. My mentor got him the lowest possible rate and a ton of options. It was everything the guy wanted.

But, he also said he *"wanted to sleep on it."*

My mentor gave no pressure and said the offer would be waiting for him.

After about a week with no word my mentor called the man to follow up. The man told him that he had decided to buy another Mercedes instead. Since my mentor had created good rapport with the man, he used this rapport to find out more.

It turned out that the Mercedes the man had bought was more expensive then the BMW. It had less room for the man's family. It had fewer features.

And the interest rate and monthly payments were higher than the BMW would have been.

My mentor was thoroughly confused, so he kept digging. When they finally got down to *the* thing that had made up the man's mind my mentor was in shock!

The man said that the Mercedes dealership was on the road between his home and his office. So, if he ever had to bring it in for repairs, he wouldn't have to go out of his way. And since he had owned a Mercedes for the past several years, he was used to doing things that way.

Coming to my mentor's dealership would have meant an extra five minutes of travel if the man had ever needed repairs. That was it.

Once the man realized what he had done he felt silly...

But by then it was too late!

The point is that people tend to design their patterns to fit around their issues. Solving their problems, though wonderful as a concept, also has another built-in component that people automatically resist...Change.

The most elegant of my GURUS mentors would recognize this kind of situation and overcome it. Not by drawing the client's attention to it and trying to browbeat them, but by showing them their limitless potential.

When you take someone beyond today and help them experience a world where their issue is gone and they have more than they currently hope for (in their current limited mindset), they will find inspiration to act and even ask for change happily.

Of course, building up from the first hello to "All this can be yours" takes some time and communication. Let's explore the various ways to get there.

☑ DO... Start a War

"The war on drugs." "The war on poverty." "The war on illiteracy." When political and pseudo-political folks want to get people motivated behind a cause they create a "war."

No one enjoys bloodshed, but…

Everyone loves to fight for what's right!

It's part of our human condition, an inborn instinct to fight for what we believe in.

The same holds true for your clients…and then some. Your clients have been "hurting" with their problem for a while. They have wanted to fight back against the problem but were unable to until you showed them how. Now it's time to rally the troops.

You see…

A cause is far more motivating than a solution!"

Your clients are human (hopefully!). And as humans we want to be more than we have been previously. We want to bring out a bigger, better, more powerful version of ourselves. As Abraham Maslow put it, we want to self-actualize.

There is no easier or faster way to do this than to start a cause. We literally become a "cause set in motion." And causes are active while solutions are passive.

Now you might ask, "How do I get my client to start a cause?" Or "How do I start a cause for my client?"

The answer is actually quite simple. What does your client stand for or against? And how does what your client's company does enable them to "fight?"

Example: Let's say you have a prospect who owns a clothing company and you sell waste management services.

As you get to know them you discover that they use organic material for their fashions. They don't believe in synthetic material because it creates harmful waste. They also only outsource to factories that work in the USA.

They want to help their home country.

At this point you can create the *cause*. The cause is to save the USA. They want to help their country and reduce harmful chemicals.

You can show them that your company also stands for building jobs at home, by only using dumps and recycling firms in the USA which creates jobs, and that you only use green-friendly waste elimination and recycling technologies.

You are united in your "war" against off-shoring and pollutants!

As you can see, the desire to "go to war" is far more powerful than simply asking the client to buy your solution. When you try to sell a solution, the solution is the focal point that must be considered, pondered and debated. When you ask your client to "go to war" your solution becomes a de facto necessity, like ammunition, uniforms or trucks.

And the best part of all is that no one has to get hurt for you to get the sale or for your client to win the war!

☑ DO... Make the Client Think for Themselves

Every morning I have a power shake. It includes eggs, a banana, ice, a tomato, celery, blueberries, strawberries, kefir, apple juice and water.

Obviously, it takes some work to put it together as is.

However, my daughter (who is four) likes to drink some of the shake too. To that end, she now has to help me put the shake together. So, a process that used to take me five minutes now takes about ten because my daughter needs more time than I do to put it together. She enjoys making her own breakfast.

In the same way clients also enjoy being involved. They are constantly bombarded by salespeople who draw out their problems and offer them ready-made solutions. And though you may think that is what clients want...solutions in a hurry...it is rarely ever the case.

Why, you ask? Because...

All humans like to have a sense of control over their destiny!

It's just like my daughter with her shake. When you put everything pre-built on a platter for them, even though it is convenient, it is not self-controlled.

So, an easy way to bypass this lack of control on the part of the client is to make them work for their solution. After you have disconnected their pain from their problem and then gotten to the lynchpin problem, ask them to create their own solution or, even better, to lay out all their own options.

Then ask them to describe the perfect solution as they see it.

How long would it take? What resources would be needed? How soon to begin? What budget would be needed? What skills, abilities, resources would be needed that they do not have available in-house, etc?

The client is now handing YOU the solution on a silver platter.

They are telling you, in no uncertain terms, what they desire. All you have to do is sit back, take notes and put it on the purchase order.

☑ DO... Find the Undiscovered Country

As one my GURUS mentors once told me, "In order for people to think about anything, they automatically think in limitation."

In other words, if you are training for a marathon and you ran six miles yesterday and today you are planning on running six-point-five miles, you are telling yourself that six-point-five is your limit today. And yet, your body may easily be able to do eight or ten or fifteen miles. But since you started with a limited number of miles you also limit how many you can do as you "grow."

It is no different in sales with clients. If your client says they want to drive up their revenue by producing 20% more widgets by year's end that is great.

And yet, what if they could do 30% or 60% more? What if they could start a new division and refurbish widgets? What if they could send out people to consult with companies to better use their widgets? What if, instead of just building the widget, they also built the machines in which the widgets were used? What if they used different materials to make the widgets and saved themselves millions in production costs…?

As you can see, once you go up to the 1,000-foot view a myriad of possibilities begins to open up for your client and, as a by-product, for you.

You stop being just a salesperson and become an explorer.

You see what is over the horizon and you show it to them. You move them beyond their limiting thoughts. You get them excited about their future!

And, just like with Christopher Columbus or Marco Polo, no one would dare dream of leaving port without their fearless leader… who just happens to be you!

CHAPTER 11
<u>BE</u> LIKE WATER

"Empty your mind, be formless, shapeless - like water. Now you put water into a cup, it becomes the cup, you put water into a bottle, it becomes the bottle, you put it in a teapot it becomes the teapot. Now water can flow or it can crash. Be water, my friend." – Bruce Lee

Many clients ask me how to handle objections. I tell them that they first have to wet themselves. After they nervously tell me that they can't see any reason to soil their pants in front of their clients, I assure them that was not what I was talking about.

I am talking about BEing like water.

Clients throw up objections consciously and unconsciously. Whether or not the objection stops you in your tracks or is effortlessly overcome does not depend upon the objection. It depends entirely on how you respond to it.

Let's picture an objection like a wall in the middle of a road. If you see yourself as a rolling stone (something that is hard and solid), your forward progress will end at the wall.

However, if you see yourself as water, then you can flow around the wall on one side or the other, whichever is the path of least resistance. Or, if the wall is blocking the whole road then, as flowing water does over time, you can build up higher and higher until you simply wash over the wall and again head on your way.

Objections, like the other obstacles we encounter in life, are not an end. They merely signal that we must adjust course.

In this chapter we'll explore objections in depth and discuss how you can **flow** by them.

☑ DO... Long for Objections

We all dream of being able to simply walk into a client's office, have a little chit chat, get to their deep problem, offer our solution and walk out with a signed purchase order in five minutes. Yet it is impossible to get the signed purchase order without having to first deal with an objection. But the truth is…

There can be no sale without objections!

Even when people don't outwardly object at all, like when they buy a pack of gum from a delicatessen, there is still an objection. The person saw the gum, found a need for it (bad breath perhaps), then saw the price, then objected to the price in their mind, or asked if their breath was really that bad, then negotiated back and forth in their mind until they decided that the gum was necessary and bought it. And all this happened in a split second!

So yes, if you are asking for a dollar or less for what you sell, you'll probably face little or no objection. But in the world of ever more complicated, B2B high end sales, objections will pop up and *must* pop up to close the deal.

There are three reasons why you <u>must</u> have objections to close deals: Trust, Rapport and Alignment

First, when a client throws up an objection they are looking to see how you respond. If you slam back against them – like stone to stone – that will break their trust in you.

But, if you flow with them and their thinking, you will strengthen their trust in you and to ultimately buy from you. They will know that you are on their side, not your own. Because for you to have your own side, you must in some way be *against* them. You are an opponent!

Second, as you work with the client to understand and deconstruct the objection, you will have to communicate with them.

As you effectively communicate with them you will increase your rapport with them. The more rapport they have with you, the more time, energy and ultimately money they will want to spend with you as well. They feel like a friend toward you and they enjoy being around you.

Third…

Objections are a symptom of lack of alignment between your idea of a situation and the client's.

The client is not objecting to you or your solution; they are objecting to their own disconnect. The reality you are presenting to them and the reality they know are not fully aligned yet. Working through the objection allows the two of you to create that perfect alignment.

And, at the end of the day, remember that clients ultimately want to solve their problems as much as…if not more than…you do. So, even though they may consciously throw up objections to stump you…

They want you to overcome their objections!

They want you to help them in spite of themselves.

☑ DO… BARF When You Hear Objections

When most salespeople hear an objection they get thrown off and even feel a little queasy, especially if the objection is truly unforeseen.

At this point the tendency, if the objection is expected, is to go into the pre-rehearsed counter to the objection. And this will work for low level sales, but is not highly regarded by the higher end buyer.

The other usual outcome, if the objection is unforeseen, is for the salesperson to get stumped and to default to "I'll look into that" or "I'll get some more information" to the client, and then politely haul ass out of Dodge and look for shelter.

The truth is that you should follow your gut reaction and BARF!

Now, I am not saying that you should spew your lunch all over the client, although that might be funny!

I am saying that you should use the GURUS method of objection handling: BARF

BARF stands for:

- Break down the objection
- Address the base issue
- Resolve the base issue
- Future test

How-To: BARF on Objections

1. Break down the objection. Remember that "peoples' biggest problem is they don't know what their biggest problem is." In that vein, "The client's biggest objection is that they don't know what they are objecting to."

   When a client objects they are trying to bring attention to the misalignment between what you are saying and what they are thinking. Yet because there are so many layers and levels to aligning, the client almost never nails down their true objection. They give you, in essence, a level 1 or 2 objection.

   It is your job to go to the deeper base issue behind the objection.

   Example: The client says, "It's too expensive."

   Common (i.e. bad) response: "Why do you say that?" This nondescript response allows the client to engage their imagination and run on with "reasons."

   A GURUS response: "It's 'too expensive' based on what?" or "In what way exactly is it 'too expensive?'"

The client is now forced to start breaking down their objection. They will come back with something like, "Well, your solution is twice our remaining budget."

As you can see we now know the real objection was *their* budget, not *our* price. That change in perspective will already start to dissolve the objection's power.

GURUS TWEAK: Use "I agree", "I appreciate" or "I respect" to start your breakdown of the objection and you will take even more pressure off the client.

"I agree. It *is* too expensive if you look at it like…"

When the client feels that you agree with them they will be even more open and responsive to you.

2. Address the base issue. At this point you very quickly want to find out how the base issue is limiting the client from engaging your solution.

   Example: You can say, "So you want the solution we've put together. You just can't afford it. Is that correct?"

   The client will say something like, "Yes. Unfortunately we don't have the full budget for your solution this year."

   We have now solidified that budget is the base issue. If it wasn't, then we would need to dig deeper until we found the real base issue.

3. Resolve the base issue. Now that you have gotten to the limiting factors at the heart of the base issue you simply need to solve it, just like you would any other problem the client is having.

   Example: You can say, "So, if we can remodel the solution to start this year and end next year, could you allot the remainder of your budget to it this year and pay us the remainder as we complete next year?"

   The client will say something like, "Yes. If you could do that, we should be able to make it work."

   You have now resolved the base issue.

4. Future test – this is a step that virtually all salespeople miss. Just because you have solved the base issue for the client right now does not mean that they will not revive it later or that they don't still see it hanging in their future.

Therefore, you need to do a little future testing to make sure that the base issue really is 100% gone.

Example: You can say, "So, just so we're clear, you're going to give us $250,000 to start this year. And we will scale the project to end sometime next year. When you get your new budget in January, you will give us the outstanding $250,000 so that we can complete the project. Correct?"

Client: "Yes."

You: "Do you see any situation in the remaining three months of this year where you'd need some of your remaining $250,000 budget?"

Client: "No."

You: "How about next year's budget? Is the $250,000 you're about to commit possibly already earmarked for something else?"

Client: "No."

At this point you are ready to get back into the natural conversation that is the alignment process.

If, however, they should find some issue in the future that would require some of the budget they are promising you, you must overcome that issue now, before getting involved. Only then can the client freely and happily commit.

☑ DO... Expect the Indirect

Obviously we all recognize the direct objections from clients like money, time, ability, belief or desire.

However, there is a whole other set of **indirect** objections that clients have that they and you don't even realize. Let's examine some of the more common ones.

Multiple Decision-Makers

The multiple decision-maker objection is commonplace in today's market. It is born out of the incorrect belief that since "two heads are better than one", more than two heads will be even better.

The truth is that…

The more brains involved in a decision the longer it will take and the poorer it will be.

Here's why.

First, the whole affair is like a game of telephone. Usually you are dealing with one "point person." This person listens to multiple decision-makers talk to him about their perspectives on "the problem."

After the point person hears all of these versions of "the problem" he then has to combine everything he has heard in order to even begin talking to possible solution providers. He has generalized "the problem." Now the point person is looking for an answer to a problem that really does not exist.

Second, each decision-maker is not really in touch with their own problem.

Remember that "People's biggest problem is they don't know what their biggest problem is."

Therefore, when a decision-maker is asked to help make a decision they are evaluating options and trying to make that decision for a problem that is undefined, so they have no idea what is wrong or how to fix it.

They are the blind leading the blind.

Third, they are unable to reach an effective consensus.

Every decision-maker has their own agenda. They bring that with them to the decision-making process.

Ultimately, since no one can define the problem, and no one knows how to solve the undefined problem, and everyone is trying to gain something for themselves from the solution to the unknown problem, they create a cluster-f*** of epic proportions!

This means that virtually every criteria, save one, gets removed. The remaining criteria is price, so...

Lowest price wins again!

To fight the hydra that is the multiple decision-maker situation you must tackle it head-on.

How-To: Overcome Multiple Decision-Makers

1. <u>Question the validity of the group</u>. No one likes to seem impolite or demanding; yet in a multiple decision-maker situation an abrupt attitude is usually called for because one of the best things you can do for your client is to stop the speeding train of "bad decision making" in its tracks.

   By openly questioning why each member of the decision-making committee is involved, you are helping your client.

   Now, the "point person" you are dealing with may not have the authority to disband the decision-making team, but when you sufficiently point out the potential issues or outright uselessness of having certain folks on a decision-making team, they will...

   a. *Take what those people say far less seriously*

   b. *Perhaps go to the top person they can reach and explain why the group should be changed, shrunk or disbanded.*

   Either way, it works better for both of you.

2. <u>Dissect and define "the problem."</u> As I pointed out, virtually no one

on the decision-making team really knows what *the* problem is. They are all taking from their own perspectives and agendas.

Since this is the case, it is vitally necessary that you dissect the main problem into its component parts, just like you dissected a frog into its component pieces in high school biology.

At this point the group itself is beginning to see the multiple layers of misalignment and the near futility of their venture. Even if the group stays together, you have forced them to see the error of their ways and to respect your opinion.

You effectively move into "expert" status in their eyes.

3. <u>Get them to focus on one problem to solve</u>. This is pretty straightforward. After all the questioning, dissecting and defining you have done, you simply lay out the linchpin problem as you see it and seek consensus from them as to its being the problem to solve.

   This does not mean that every problem is solved, but since you've shown them that there are multiple issues to address, they will no longer be looking for a generalized solution to a generalized problem.

Fortune Telling

In straight "this for that" transactions, such as buying five gallons of gasoline for $10 at the gas station or a buying a six pack of beer for $8 at the liquor store, there is no question in the buyer's mind about what will happen when they purchase.

However, in the world of complex high end sales, clients often cannot fully comprehend the future of their decision, its outcomes or ramifications. In this situation the buyer often looks to the salesperson to tell them the future. Moreover, they usually want the salesperson to make promises that they can't really make.

Example: We have someone who sells business development consulting services. They go through the sales process with a client.

Near the end of the process the client asks the salesperson *exactly* how much more the company will make by using the service, *exactly* how long the process will take, *exactly* how much growth will happen, *exactly* what kind of growth will take place, and when *exactly* they will get back their investment so they have the capital in hand to start investing in other ventures.

As you can see, this situation puts the salesperson in a precarious position. They want to make the sale and yet they are being asked to make promised predictions that involve multiple situations over which no one has any control.

The easiest way to handle this type of objection is with two simple steps…

How-To: Overcome Requests for Fortune Telling in Two Steps

1. **Dismiss promises.** It is out of integrity to make promises you can't control or guarantee. So, even though the client may be demanding such promises, you must tell them in all honesty what you can control or guarantee and what you can't.

   So, our friend the business development consulting salesperson could say something like, "I can appreciate your concerns. Honestly, this process, like any other, can be pre-planned down to minute detail. And yet, as always, there will be situations that arise that we can't foresee. This is true of any new process. So, at best, I can give you good estimates, but I cannot guarantee exact outcomes."

   Yes, the client may choose to go with another solution-provider at that point, but you have done the best you can for the client.

   They are now risking their investment on the lies of another person. If and when things blow up in their face, the client may come back to you because at least *you* were honest.

2. **Discuss potential.** Ultimately the guarantee your client is looking

for is based on some perceived need they have for your solution to work.

This is the perfect opportunity to go into the future with them, see what they want and then talk about the outcomes your product or service can provide that are far beyond the potential they thought they had.

Again, using the business development consulting salesperson as an example, he could say, "Now, what's more far important than the first phase of outcomes is the overall increase this project will allow you to carry out for years to come.

"Since your production will now be increased by at least X and the new system can be recreated anywhere, you will be able to market and deliver your widgets into Europe and then Asia. Basically, implementing this solution means that you will be stepping into the realm of a true global company."

As the client attaches to the expanded potential of the future via your solution, they will disconnect from their "promise me this" attitude of the present, which puts the alignment process right back on track.

Stalled Momentum

One of the sneakiest indirect objections, that virtually all of my GURUS mentors warned me about, is the loss of momentum on the part of the client in the sales process. The client is used to making salespeople do "dog and pony shows" until they get enough of a clue to figure out what they want to buy.

Of course, these long processes can die of attrition.

The client gets busy with other things and the salesperson gets busy with prospects who are newer, more promising and more active.

A simple way to keep the momentum going in these situations is to politely turn the tables on the client and put them to work.

Example: Clients will regularly ask salespeople to "Gather more information on X for the next meeting." At this point the salesperson runs back to their office and gathers more paperwork to bring with them to the next meeting.

They think the paperwork is important, when in reality it is merely a delaying tactic on the part of the client.

Yet it is fair for the client to ask for more material if they feel it necessary. If you can't convince them otherwise, then turn the tables and ask them to gather more information too, such as saying, "Okay, I'll get the information you asked for. However, for it to be of any real use for consideration, I am going to need to see your company's usage levels of X for the last eight months, broken down by division."

You are subtly communicating three important realizations to the client with this move…

I.   You are their equal, not their lackey.

II. You can rationalize the need for more useless information just like they can.

III. You expect them to stay an active participant in this process.

At this point the client changes their perspective on you and, as a by-product, on your product or service. This move can win you great respect with clients; just be sure to use it wisely and not abuse it.

The Long Sales Cycle

"Long sales cycles are just par for the course in high end sales." I can't tell you how many times I have heard this line of bullshit that most salespeople use to explain their lack of sales. These same folks will also be the most likely to say, "They went with a lower-priced solution" at the eight or twelve-month mark when the buyer buys elsewhere.

If my GURUS mentors all agreed on one thing it was this:

The length of your sales cycle has only one determining factor...YOU!

If you set in your mind that your sales cycles will be long, then you will program the process to be long.

Now, to be fair, clients also exacerbate the situation by being lost. As I have said over and over, "People's biggest problem is they don't know what their biggest problem is." This lack of understanding is the monkey wrench that clients throw into the system in every "long" sales process.

They might disguise this monkey wrench of confusion as a "buying policy" or "having to run it by the board" or "needing case studies" or "having to talk to multiple bidders", etc.

In the end, any internal processes that they have created or adhere to are usually detrimental to their cause and were born out of confusion about how to make a quick and effective decision.

Now, most buyers will cling to their process like it's a holy scripture and they may even fight for it. Yet the same process easily goes right out the window when the CEO's brother gets a $1MM project with no bidding and no notice given to anyone. So...

Sales cycle lengths are completely arbitrary. Period!

This lack of clarity on the part of the client, and the desire to **push product** instead of assist the client to clarity, is what leads to long sales cycles.

Simply, sales cycles take as long as necessary until the two parties either stumblebum their way to alignment or another salesperson beats them to it. There is your "long" sales cycle decoded.

So, the way to shorten any sales cycle is to break it down just like any other objection.

The BARF system we covered earlier works perfectly here too.

How-To: BARF on Long Sales Cycles

1. Break it down. "What makes you use this system to buy?" or "How has it been working for you?" or "What would you do if these procedures didn't exist?"

2. Address the base issue. "So the reason you're using this system is because you think you'll get in trouble if you don't?" or "Then you agree that following these procedures will most likely result in a solution choice that is bad for your company?"

3. Resolve the base issue. "What if you and I did this like there were no rules and then, if you chose our solution, we'd just make the pieces retrofit into your system...if needed?" or "What if you bucked the system and made a fantastic solution choice based on how we're working together and your bosses were thrilled?"

4. Future test. "Do you see any situation in the future where this may be an issue again?" or "Do you plan on going back to this system after we start working together?"

As you can see, BARFing is always appropriate!

CHAPTER 12
<u>BE</u> EXPERIENCED

Too often salespeople look at the sales process as a series of events that are tenuously connected and are meant to drive the client to a buying decision. The truth is that everything is part of the overall *experience* for the client.

This is why "closing" is problematic for many salespeople. They make the mistake of thinking that a) the client wants to be "closed" and b) that getting the final "yes", the check in hand or the signed agreement is somehow a distinct and separate part of the process.

One of my GURUS mentors went so far as to say that...

"CLOSE is a four-letter word."

She much preferred the word "secure," because it is far more akin to what the client desires. This is because the client, unlike the salesperson, has not gone through the sales process looking to "close" it and have it be over. Instead they have been patiently building up to "secure" something of great value to them.

Therefore, when you "secure the pact", rather than "go for the close", you are already energetically coming from the same space as the client.

The client is seeking "security" in the solution and wants to trust that you will deliver it, so "pact" more accurately reflects the degree of importance you give to the relationship than just a "sale", "deal" or "arrangement."

And since sales is all about alignment, you will be continuing the momentum you have already built, rather than derailing it with a "close."

This plays into the concept of "experientializing" that many of my mentors subscribe to.

Again, the whole sales process is an *experience* for the client.

Experientializing is any point when you create a real *out-of-the-ordinary* experience for the client.

There are several ways to experientialize when you are looking to "secure the pact" with a client. Let's explore some of them.

☑ DO... Make a Movie

If you have followed the GURUS methodology up to this point, the client should already be eager to buy your product or service. If they aren't it is because...

They are excited but also misguided.

In other words, they have a desire but they don't have a system – or they don't have a *good* system – with which to make a buying decision.

Now, let's be clear. I'm not saying that they lack some two-page-long dictate that was created by someone twenty years ago, who also no longer works for the company, which outlines the procedures for purchasing products or services.

I am saying that the individual lacks an <u>internal</u> buying system. They lack the *trigger* within themselves that must be pulled to allow them to say YES to you.

So, the easiest thing is to create the joy of the *experience* of buying from you. That way they will know it is right.

How-To: The Blu-ray DVD Buying Decision Experience

Up until a few years ago the only type of DVD player available was red-ray. Though it provided a good amount of storage, it was limited in how much data it could store, how accessible the stored data was and how accurately it could be read. It also limited the capacity of High Definition picture quality.

Thanks to the newer Blu-ray technology, the same disc can now hold 100 times the same amount of information, process it faster, give better picture quality and pinpoint material more accurately.

In addition, these discs can also offer many more bonus features like deleted scenes, bloopers, different camera angles, director's commentary and multiple alternate endings. All in all a much richer experience then even the theater could provide.

Let's look at creating a decision **experience** for the buyer that's like working with a Blu-ray DVD…on steroids!

The client is at a potential decision point in choosing whether or not to use your product or service, but they are still guessing at the outcome. They want to **feel** secure in their decision. They want to know what the end result will be even though it hasn't happened yet.

This is the perfect scenario for this decision-making experience.

Rather than giving you a direct step by step, I will walk you through an example of how I use it, to demonstrate.

> Buyer: I don't know what to do.
>
> Me: Okay, let's have some fun. If that is all right with you.
>
> Buyer: Sure.
>
> Me: Okay, let's pretend for a moment that you had a Blu-ray DVD of the movie of your company's story. It starts today and goes into the future. And it is playing on a TV set right there (I point to a spot in front of the client).
>
> Buyer: All right.
>
> Me: Now I'd like you to pick up your remote and hit PLAY and see your company as it is today. (I always make sure they actually raise their hand and press the imaginary remote.)
>
> You're doing okay with A, B and C. And you are struggling with X, Y and Z. See the faces of the people you work with. See the issues that restrict them.

Buyer: Okay.

Me: Now, pick up your remote again and select FAST FORWARD. This would be fast forwarding your current state of affairs, without changing anything in your company and allowing all the current issues to continue to grow. And let's fast forward eighteen months from today.

Let me know when you're there.

Buyer: Okay. I'm there.

Me: Good. Tell me *everything* you see.

Buyer: I see us doing worse.

Me: Well, remember this is high definition we're watching. So tell me *everything* you're seeing now in vivid clarity.

Buyer: Our sales are down another 12%. We've slipped behind two more competitors and are now number six in our industry.

Me: And..?

Buyer: I've had to lay off eighteen people.

Me: Were they good people?

Buyer: All my people are good people.

Me: Okay. What else is happening?

Buyer: I've cut my own salary in half and I have stopped putting money into my 401K. I've gotten offers to sell, but the people making the offers are looking at us like vultures and are offering ridiculously low numbers.

Me: And…?

Buyer: What else do you want?

Me: How do you look?

Buyer: Tired.

Me: Okay. Now step into yourself at that moment. How do you *feel*?

Buyer: Like crap!

Me: All right. Step back out of yourself then and be watching the TV again.

Buyer: Okay.

Me: Now pick up your remote and press STOP and then REWIND. And rewind back to now.

Buyer: Okay. Done.

Me: Great! Now press MENU and select ALTERNATE ENDINGS

Buyer: Okay.

Me: Now select the ending you told me you want. The one where you increase sales by at least 2% per month and add new lead generation processes on a regular basis.

Buyer: Okay.

Me: Hit PLAY, then fast forward to eighteen months again.

Buyer: Okay.

Me: Tell me what you see.

Buyer: Everything is great!

Me: Remember, "High definition." More details. Where are you? What are you doing?

Buyer: I'm in my office. I am looking at the sales figures for the last quarter. We have closed over $200MM in sales.

Me: And...?

Buyer: And I call the CFO to discuss awarding bonuses while I pull out the Cuban cigar I have been saving for a special occasion and light up.

Me: Fantastic! Now step into the TV and into yourself in that moment now. How do you feel?

Buyer: Pretty goddamn cool!

Me: Excellent! Now I want you to step back out and be watching the TV again. Pick up your remote and hit REWIND so you can watch the images as they rewind. And I want you to rewind the movie back to point where it changed. Rewind back to the point now where you made a decision that completely changed everything and created this ending for the movie.

Buyer: I guess it's now. It's this.

Me: There is no need to guess. You have the DVD. The moment is right there in front of you now. So what was it? What was the decision?

Buyer: It's now. It is working with you.

Me: Positive?

Buyer: Yes!

Me: Great! Then let's make that movie happen!

Buyer: Where do I sign?

Obviously this is a best case scenario demonstration. Nonetheless, you can see the Blu-Ray DVD decision process at work and reconstruct it for yourself.

And, in case you're not sure how it goes, simply rewind to the beginning of this section and start again…after all, it's right there in front of you now!

☑ DO… Give the Client a Quickie

Sometimes the client is so overcome or overwhelmed in their current situation that all they want to get the sale moving is some immediate relief. Obviously, you can't solve all of the client's issues right there on the spot. But if you can give just a little quick gratification…

The client will simply go right into the process and never look back!

The compulsion to buy, in this case the compulsion to buy your solution, is driven by instant gratification. But only the client can create within themselves the *experience* that will create that compulsion.

This is why alignment is imperative. It is the only way that you can be in the same space as the client and affect their internal atmosphere enough to connect their UBP to your quick gratification solution so they are compelled to buy.

In order to give the client a "quickie" you simply need to set up a "flip the switch" step that is the first thing that happens to them or for them once they buy from you.

Example: One of my clients is a high end consulting firm that specializes in cost reduction for manufacturing companies. They have a four-person sales team.

One day I was out doing some field observation on one of their senior salespeople, a very personable woman with an amazingly tactical mind. She was having her third meeting with the COO of a large manufacturing company with plants all over North America.

She was doing her standard song and dance, and he was giving her the usual polite runaround. He politely talked about her competitors. She politely tried to squash those thoughts. It was all very polite.

At one point he mentioned, almost offhandedly, how much transportation costs were an issue for them. When he mentioned this point I saw a change come over his face for a moment, and then it was gone.

But it was too late.

She had seen his "pain" face, and that was all she needed.

She spent the rest of the conversation asking and digging about their transportation costs and issues. There were many transportation problems and cost overrun issues, but the main one, the one his boss had been giving him the hardest time about, had to do with their steel shipping costs from the Midwest and Canada.

To his defense, he had been handling many other operational "fires" that had required his attention. But the CFO and the CEO, a stickler for numbers, just wouldn't stop riding him about these particular costs. It needed to be handled, but he just didn't have the time and resources to address it right then.

My colleague, and every other salesperson from every other cost reduction firm that had come to see this COO, had been pitching him on a company-wide, top-to-bottom project scope. His resistance to going so big so fast was evident, but so was his pain about the steel shipping costs.

In short order my colleague dropped the big project concept and simply said that her firm would just work on the steel transport issues. And, if that went well, they would discuss further projects.

The cost was paltry and they'd barely break even on the project, but she didn't care. She knew that all he needed was to have one quick gratification and he would be back for more.

It worked. Less than a week later he signed the agreement for the micro-project. My client's firm kicked ass, fast! The COO was happy, which meant the CFO and CEO were also happy. And my client's firm is now handling multiple projects at most of their facilities in the USA.

As you can see...

The quickie was enough to compel the client to buy and buy again.

Another great by-product of the instant gratification situation is that it sets things up so the only way the client can get their instant gratification is to sign with you.

So you are compassionately assisting them in making a decision that benefits them and allowing them to sample that great decision immediately, which eliminates buyer's remorse and creates a desire for the rest of the solution that will follow.

☑ DO... A Gut Check

Oftentimes, when you get to the moment where you present the client with a buying decision, the buyer seems to hesitate. This has nothing to do with you. So long as you have followed all the steps in the GURUS process, you have certainly presented the client with the best solution for them.

What is happening is that the client is internally disconnected. They haven't connected to a buying decision location within themselves.

Remember that there are three types of buying decisions...

I. Brain-based. This is the logical type of decision, which is born from choosing the "best" of what has been offered. It usually follows a long sales process, and usually comes down to the cheapest price and doesn't thrill either the buyer or seller. It's just a decision that "had to be made." (Poor decision)

II. Heart-based. This is the purely emotional decision, which is born from an extreme emotional occurrence (most likely fear) coupled with a "do something now" situation. The buyer is never happy with this decision, even if it was the best one, and it will ultimately result in buyer's remorse. (Poor decision)

III. Gut-based. This is the feeling-based decision, which is born from a fluid experience between the salesperson and buyer. The buyer agrees to buy without having to do the micro-detail check of the brain-based decision and without any of the remorse of the heart-based decision. (Best decision)

When the client is internally disconnected, the simple solution is to do a *gut check*.

Get the client to connect with their gut...literally!

I simply tell the client to temporarily put aside the chatter that their brain is throwing at them and the emotional roller coaster that their heart wants them to ride on. After I have gotten them to a place of temporary calm, I tell them to ask their gut what to do.

Example of what I'd say: OK, Jack. Our guts never lie to us. They are the wise mediators between our hearts and minds. And since they want to keep eating, they will always make the decision that assures they will get the most meals. That means it will be the decision that has the best ROI for you. So, with that in mind, take a look at your gut. (Client looks at belly). Now ask your gut, "Does it feel right to you to buy X now?"

The client may feel a little foolish or awkward, and you may have to coach them a little to get them to really "talk" with their gut, but it works! Personally, I have never had a client balk at this process and I have secured many pacts and created many satisfied clients with this technique.

☑ DO... Perturb the Client

> *per·turb (verb) 1. to disturb or disquiet greatly in mind; agitate. 2. to throw into great disorder; derange.*

Years ago I attended a seminar hosted by Blair Singer, author of *Sales Dogs*. He taught me how to do stage presentations and group trainings. We worked with a technology called *Accelerated Learning*.

Blair taught us that to really learn something in a short period of time, the audience members had to have a rapid *internal* experience that would create irreversible change inside of them.

To explain his point, Blair talked about Ilya Prigogine, the *Second Law of Thermo-Dynamics* and the *Theory of Dissipative Structures*.

Thankfully, you don't have to know all the physics and psychology we discussed that week. All you have to know is the story of the tree in the swamp.

You see, when a tree falls into a swamp, it's instantly taken out of its usual environment. It used to have its roots in the ground, grow toward the sky, and take in carbon dioxide and give out oxygen through photosynthesis.

Now it is lying horizontal under several feet of water. Life as the tree knew it is over.

As time goes on, the tree is pressured by the weight of the water, and it soaks in the minerals from the water. Over time the elements in the water begin to interact with the elements in the tree at the atomic level. These tiny chemical reactions give off heat and energy.

The tree is being perturbed!

At this point the tree can go only one of two ways. Either the chemical reactions will cause the tree to disintegrate, or the tree's atoms will reorganize themselves to handle the new environment.

And then, in a flash of light and heat, the tree's atoms reorganize themselves and crystallize. A petrified tree is created, which can easily handle the swampy environment.

When you have been dealing with a client about a serious problem, and they have been "pressured" from all sides to solve the problem, they have been going through their own perturbation as they've gone through the sales process with you.

With this understanding you may feel the desire to "ease up" on the client.

That would be a disservice to the client!

Remember that you don't **need** the sale. You only **want** to help the client. And if that means pushing the client to their breaking/change point, so be it.

Now, if you do this as a "closing tactic" you will lose credibility and respect from the client.

However, if done the GURUS way, as a friend who cares about the client more than the sale, you will become their ally. And people will do anything for their allies!

☑ DO… Make Only Perfunctory Proposals

Sometimes you get to the buying decision point just to be met with "Can you put that into a proposal for me?"

Most salespeople fear that if they push back or state the obvious - "We've already discussed everything to death" - the client will balk and walk. So they grudgingly say Yes, knowing that they've just been dumped back into the waiting game.

The truth is that…

Asking for a proposal at this stage is just another objection!

The client still hasn't "bought" the experience of working with you and your solution. In other words, they are still shopping, because proposals don't sell, they just sit.

So, how do we bypass the "proposal" issue? Simple: Make a perfunctory proposal right there.

When I am asked for a proposal at the buying decision moment, I politely tell the client that I don't really like proposals and I will list my reasons. Then I will suggest that we quickly review everything and put it on paper right then.

Since the client isn't really expecting this, and they have no backup excuse, they usually agree.

How-To: Handle Proposal Requests

1. Cover the problem that has to be solved and get agreement on its severity from the client.

2. Cover the solution to be implemented and get agreement on its validity and value from the client.

3. Cover the fee, timetable, milestones, guarantees and any other bits and pieces that would be needed for a formal agreement. As

you do this, <u>write</u> it down!

4. Get the client to agree that this is the solution for them.

   a. *If you have a formal agreement ready, fill in the blanks and get the client to sign it.*

   b. *If you don't have a formal agreement handy, add "Typed agreement to be delivered within 48 hours" to the written proposal and then photocopy it.*

5. Sign your handwritten original and the photocopy.

6. Take the original and a check for a 10% deposit on the agreed-upon fees. The remainder of the fee(s) is due when the typed contract is delivered by FedEx the next day.

NOTE: When putting together proposals, agreements, etc., do yourself a favor and make the language as easy to understand as possible. Yes, everybody loves "airtight" agreements, but hardcore legal jargon can also turn an agreed-upon sale into a nit-picky nightmare that can ultimately lose the sale. So, make your agreements as simple as possible.

☑ DO... Laugh at RFP's

Yes, I know RFP's have nothing to do with the experience of "securing the pact" with clients, and are usually a torture test placed at the beginning of any buying process that uses them. However, since we just covered proposals, I felt this would be an appropriate place to discuss RFPs.

I did one RFP in my life. It was time-consuming, annoying and ultimately a rip-off because the buyer had already chosen the vendor they wanted. They were just getting the five competing RFPs they needed (Have to do things by the book, you know) before they could award the project to their friend.

So, I highly recommend that you avoid doing RFPs, unless your company has a long history of generating and securing projects via RFP with the same buyer who is requesting it. In that case, why break with tradition?

Or, if you know your cost will be far and away the cheapest, then knock yourself out.

All others beware!

Now, if you still find yourself in an RFP position and it is required (by your boss) to be handled, here is what I would do.

How-To: Deal with RFPs...If You Must

1. Call the buyer and tell them straight out that the RFP is a waste of time.

2. Explain that you can't possibly make a proposal blind, and that the description in the RFP has left you with more questions than answers.

3. Tell them that they will most likely get a subpar product or service by using their RFP.

4. Use the opportunity to begin asking them some of the questions you have. You can then use this to create rapport, align with them and ultimately get to their unique buying position. You know the rest from there.

If you find that there is no UBP on their part, you will know that this is either a "tire kicker" RFP or that they have already made their vendor choice and they just want to waste your time to fulfill their paperwork requirements.

At this point feel free to laugh and hang up!

SECTION FOUR

How do <u>GURUS</u> create more sales from their clients and contacts?

Be Do Sale

Chapter 13
<u>BE</u> an Ally

There seems to be a preoccupation among many high end salespeople out there with trying to become "trusted advisers" to their clients so they can continue to do business with the clients again and again. Although I understand and agree with the basic idea of the concept, I would also say that…

Trying to be a trusted adviser is a waste of time!

As an "adviser" your comments *may* be taken under consideration. Of course, most elite clients have several advisers or, as in the case of CXO's, too many advisers. So your comments will only be as valuable as the others'. This means that your input risks getting lost in the "turf wars" of the inner sanctum of your client's company.

Instead I recommend you make yourself an "ally" to your clients. Now, your first thought might be that I am simply playing semantics here, but trust me, I'm not.

As I discussed earlier in the section *DO…Start a War*, you want to create a "cause" for your client to believe in or a "fight" against something for them to engage in. When you do this the entire dynamic between you and the client changes. You become allies, which is far more important and primordial than an "adviser."

During World War Two President Roosevelt and Prime Minister Churchill both had plenty of advisers. But in the end, when one of the allies moved, the other went with him, come hell or high water. There was something greater than any individual desires at stake. The fate of the world rested on sticking together and acting as one.

The fate of your client's world rests on sticking together with you!

As an ally your thoughts, words and actions take on a far greater meaning to the client. They will begin to act in unison with you, so long as you remember to put *their* needs first.

As you may remember, there was a third "ally" in World War Two. Joseph Stalin and the USSR were allies of the USA and UK, but only so long as it served their needs. Once the war was over, so was the alliance. So Stalin was truly just an opportunist, not an ally.

But the USA and UK are still allies, and move in unison with each other to this day. They are true allies.

Being an ally to your clients will create all of the additional sales, etc. that you want to generate with your clients. Of course, dealing with this alliance is different than dealing with the run-of-the-mill CRM methods that most sales systems espouse. Following are some of the ways to DO alliances the GURUS way.

☑ DO… Found a Cult

Cults get a bad rap. The only time we seem to be aware of a cult is when the FBI is storming their fortified compound or bringing their leader to trial. But defining cults by this idea is the same as saying because one of the apples in the orchard is bad we should forget the whole crop this year.

Honestly, a "cult" is not only a group of extreme religious folk with more guns than brains. It can also define any group of sane individuals who are allied in their devotion to a person, concept or movement.

So in truth…

All religions and political parties are technically cults.

Maybe that's why we don't discuss them with people we want to be friends with…

Now, Jeffrey Gitomer says, "Customer satisfaction is worthless. Customer loyalty is priceless."

I agree, with an addendum: Customer loyalty to you or your solution doesn't mean more sales. But client **alliance** with you **for** something or **against** something does.

This is where the power of the cult comes to life. When there is something bigger to believe in, live for, fight against, people will continue to be active in their belief.

This is why people go to church, vote for **their** party, volunteer to assist charities, and why "cool" people buy anything **Apple** makes. They are allied with others in their belief and they perpetuate it on a regular basis.

What's more, the truly devoted will go above and beyond and propagate their beliefs, like Jehovah's Witnesses at your door, political aides handing out flyers, or the brave souls who are volunteer firemen.

So, instead of looking to create customer loyalty to you or your product, lead the cult that stands for or against something with your client. Then it becomes based in themselves. It is inspirational, and it moves them to continuous activity because it is aligned with their core.

And what is the easiest way for them to do that "continuous activity?" Well, to buy more from you, of course!

☑ DO... Tweak How You Get Referrals

I have tried my hand at many careers in my lifetime. I have been or have tried to be an actor, a houseman, a records manager, a karate teacher, a management consultant, a busboy, a screenwriter, a real estate investor, a dishwasher, a fitness trainer, a contractor, a housekeeper, a deal broker, an advertising designer, a warehouseman, an office services consultant, a network marketer, and many other things.

But the first time I really started a business and had any clue what I was doing was when I started my professional organizing company.

I had two things going for me when I started in the industry that gave me an advantage.

First, I was a man in a female-dominated industry, so clients who had needs that included fixing stuff and building stuff tended to choose me.

Second, I never told people that how they organized was "wrong." I simply asked them what they wanted and worked with them to make it happen as painlessly as possible, while allowing them to basically keep doing what they were doing with a few little tweaks.

Of course…

The life blood of any business owner or salesperson is new leads.

Obviously one of the best ways to get new leads is by referral. And here too I "tweaked" some things that proved to be highly profitable for me… and now for you as well!

Most salespeople are similar to service professionals in how they ask for referrals. They wait until the project is over or the product is delivered. Then they wait a day or a week or a month and call the client and ask if they know anyone else who can use their product or service.

The client stammers out something like, "I'll let you know" and quickly makes their good-byes. Game over.

Two little tweaks I made to this system increased my referral rate by over 300% in less than a month, so only use them if you *really* want more referrals.

How-To: Add Two Tweaks to Your Referral System

1. Don't wait until the work is done or the product is delivered, in use and already accepted as status quo to ask for a referral. Ask for a referral at the moment of deepest impact for the client. This is the moment when the client is feeling it the most.

   Example: In my organizing days I would wait until the client and I had cleaned out the most important or the most congested room, whatever room the client really wanted to get back in control of. As soon as the last box was stored or the last book shelved, I would have the client stop and "behold" the room. They would see, sense and feel how amazing the work we were doing was. *This* is when I would ask for referrals.

2. Do not ask, "Do you know anyone…?" Instead ask, "Who are two or three people….?" When you ask the client if they know anyone who can use your solution their subconscious mind will say no because it is seeking the path of least resistance. The mind doesn't work any harder than it has to. If no one your client knows has expressly come up to them and said, "I need X", then the client's mind is telling the truth. It doesn't know anyone who would want your solution.

   When you ask the client, "Who are two or three people you know that can use my solution right now?" that is a different question. Now the mind has to examine everyone it knows. It has to evaluate them and their situations to see if it thinks any of them needs your product or service.

   Also, because the mind likes to feel that it has a choice and it likes the path of least resistance, being asked if it knows "two or three people", it can automatically default to giving you only two names and still fulfill what was asked of it. Of course, you still get two solid leads…so it was a victory all around!

☑ DO… Make It Easy to Refer You

Sometimes clients may have personal or technical restrictions that keep them from being able to directly refer you to the friends, family or colleagues. They will readily raise these limitations as a defense to your referral request.

Of course, if you have followed the other GURUS steps…

You already have a way around this!

By building your Unique Sales Persona and establishing your credibility and authority position and utilizing multiple media, such as blogs, articles or videos, you have a wealth of existing information items that you can tell your clients to direct their friends, family and colleagues to.

In this way they can refer your brilliance without having to directly refer your product or service.

Everyone is happy and no one gets in trouble.

☑ DO... Get Angry

Sometimes you've just got to get angry to get a referral!

A few years ago I helped create an association of elite consultants that service middle-market companies worldwide.

After a few months one of the members came to me and said that he had been doing his part and regularly referring his clients to two other members of the group. They, in turn, had parlayed these referrals into hundreds of thousands of dollars in business. But they had not been returning the favor of referrals.

Though our unwritten understanding was that everyone should refer other members as often as possible, it was not a requirement and was, therefore, unenforceable.

Of course, that didn't mean he couldn't force it.

I told my concerned colleague to be very direct with the other two members, and to lay it on the line.

I directed him to tell them that he had many more folks to refer them to, which he did, and to tell them that he was expecting at least one well-qualified lead from them for every one he gave them. And I also told him to tell them that if they didn't want to play that way, then he would take his leads to other folks that would.

Needless to say…

They gladly played his game.

Some people said that my "tit for tat" directions went against the spirit of the group. To this I politely said: Screw that idea!

Members who greedily **sucked from the tit** without giving back truly broke the spirit of the group. All I was doing was helping my colleague restore some balance.

☑ DO… Create Your Own Testimonials

Though I am not big on using testimonials in my sales process, I understand that some folks want to gather and use as many of them as possible. And that's fine. Of course, the big question is…

Do those testimonials have any use?

The truth is that if you have twenty testimonials but all they say is "John's a nice guy", they aren't going to make connections or create sales.

The big mistake is to assume that your clients know how to write a persuasive testimonial.

Now, there are some of you reading who already know this, but who also feel it is impolite to offer a ready-made testimonial for your clients to sign. Or, worse, you do of s you need to ask the client (or yourself) for a great testimonial…

I.   What pain or problem were you experiencing before we solved it? Get to as deep a level as possible and be as specific as possible.

II. Did you try other solutions? How did they work?

III. How many other solutions did you look at?

IV. What impressed you most about our product or service?

V. What was different about us and/or our solution?

VI. Where are you now and where would you be if you hadn't used our solution?

VII. Now that you know the value of this solution, how much do you feel it is worth or how much $$$ value did it deliver?

VIII. What would you say to anyone who is currently in the same situation you were in before?

Again, these are the questions you should ask your client. But as I said, you may also need to ask these questions of "yourself." This is because oftentimes the client can't articulate what the real answers to these questions are. As the objective outsider, you often have the best perspective. So, don't be afraid to add to your client's responses.

Another thing to keep in mind is that...

You should limit your testimonials.

If you put too many testimonials somewhere, most will go unread (or unwatched or unheard if you are using video or audio). So for things like brochures or web pages, I recommend no more than three testimonials. For business cards, I recommend no more than one testimonial.

Also remember, just like with your other Smarketing messages, that you keep in mind who you intend to see, hear or read the testimonial before you design it.

You must always remember that a testimonial, like any other message, must be designed with the prospect in mind.

☑ DO...Choose Continuous Solving Over Cross-Selling

Pretty much every time I am called in to work with sales teams one of the main questions they have is, "How can I cross-sell (or up-sell) clients?"

My response: "You can't."

Cross-selling does not exist!

It is mistakenly based in the construct that because a client has bought Solution A from you they will now be interested in Solution B. That is never the case.

Remember that your clients care about themselves and their needs first and foremost. Once they have bought your solution they need a chance to see how it works and to *feel* that it works for them. At that point all the credibility you leveraged up front is now secured. Before that, you are just plucking an ever-tightening guitar string.

Most sales trainers tell their students to start "cross-selling" as soon as the first deal is inked. Big mistake!

Let's look at this from the buyer's side. The buyer has just gone through a sales process with you. Even if it was short, it was still trying on them because they had to accept some truths they didn't know or didn't want to know. They feel good about the solution they have agreed to and they are ready to implement it and watch it bear fruit.

As they are signing the agreement they are at the point of overwhelm and they are looking forward to deflating a little after this process and integrating your solution into their business life and "getting back to normal."

If, at this stage, you start talking to them about other problems, you will push them beyond their saturation point. Instead of viewing you as an ally they will now begin to associate you with the "pain" in their head your words are causing.

Your welcome is then revoked!

The truth is that once you solve one problem there is always another waiting to take the number one spot. But just like any process of growth or change, the person has to adjust to their new environment and new way of being before they can handle more.

The simple solution? A little bit of patience.

There will be more than enough chances for you to help your client further and create more sales. The key thing to remember is that when another problem takes over as number one...

The client will be looking for solutions from you... not sales to you.

You have already set up a bigger, brighter future with the client as you discussed the **undiscovered country**. The client wants that future, and they will let you know when the next step toward it comes along.

And since you are already aligned with the client you don't need to go through the whole process again. You can simply reengage at the rapport point and go through UBP to create another solution and sale. And the process will be much faster and easier each time you do it.

Just don't lose the race by jumping the gun!

☑ DO...Remain a Factor

Once you have become a sales ally with your clients you are left walking a path that must be trod carefully. You must remember that "Familiarity breeds contempt", but also "Out of sight, out of mind." Therefore, you must stay in the client's current sphere of thought while not accidentally invading it.

Obviously, you've heard of having a "continuation" or "follow-up" system for clients and contacts. And you've probably also heard that you should do a newsletter and put everyone on the mailing list, while making sure to send the occasional special news item, etc. to more valuable clients. And while this is the standard, and a nice idea…

It doesn't really work.

Most salespeople subscribe their clients to the newsletter their company puts out on a monthly or quarterly basis. The first problem with this is that the schedule gap in communication time is enough for you to fall out of mind.

The second problem is that the content of the newsletter is generalized to speak to all the types of clients the company has, so it really speaks to no one.

The third problem is that the newsletter just conveys data and doesn't reconnect the client to you, their wonderful sales ally.

As for the occasional news piece that is "pertinent" to a client, this again falls into the realm of giving the client data, but not connecting them to you.

Instead of thinking of this as a "continuation" or "follow-up" system, try looking at it as a "never-ending challenge" system.

Remember that step two of GURUS is the Unique Sales Persona. This is the phase for when you make yourself compelling to clients. Of course, if you talked about problems they didn't have, they wouldn't have contacted you. So the secret is that…

You must continually remind your clients of their challenges.

This doesn't happen with blah-blah newsletters or the odd news piece.

So the easiest thing to do is just what you already do. If you are already using a blog or videos, etc. to put your voice out there and draw attention to the issues your clients have, simply keep doing it. And just make sure that you send the links to your clients and colleagues.

In this way you are A) killing two birds with one stone...getting old and new clients; B) staying in the awareness of your clients; and C) reminding current and past clients of the potential challenges they now face that you can help with.

So really, your "follow-up" strategy is the same as your lead generation strategy! The only difference is that your existing clients have a deeper knowledge of you, so when they hear your opinion, ideas, etc., the words have a greater impact on them because it is their ally speaking.

Thus you've set up your "follow-up" already. Congrats!

Epilogue – BE DO SALE

If there is a "spiritual archetype" for *The GURUS Selling System*, it is Bruce Lee.

Bruce Lee is revered around the world as the epitome of martial arts mastery. No one has ever claimed to be better than him. And, since he is gone, no one will ever be able to.

The funny thing is that Bruce Lee never even earned a black belt. He got to brown belt level, just shy of black, with his first kung-fu teacher, Yip Man. He then left for America.

After coming to America, Bruce started to learn techniques from other martial arts systems. He incorporated what worked for him and forgot the rest. (To quote him, "Use what is useful. Discard what is useless.")

Ultimately, Bruce created his own martial arts system called Jeet Kune Do (Way of the Intercepting Fist). This is the system he used to become the best martial artist in the world. And though there are tons of schools in the world that teach Jeet Kune Do, you will never be able to learn it.

You see, even when Bruce was alive and teaching students like Steve McQueen and Kareem Abdul Jabar, he would explain that Jeet Kune Do was *his* style. It was how his body did martial arts, so no one else would ever be able to do it.

He could teach his students techniques, but in the end they would have to create their *own* personal style, their *own* Jeet Kune Do.

It all started with Bruce's students BEing great martial artists in their hearts and minds. Then their bodies could DO whatever was best for them based upon the techniques they could use. Eventually they were able to HAVE their own personal martial arts systems.

They created their *own* Jeet Kune Do.

This is what I hope I have done with you.

GURUS is the result of what I have learned in my work with the greatest salespeople and marketers in the world. Like Bruce Lee I have used what was useful and discarded what was useless. And I have presented it here for you.

I encourage you to take the concepts and techniques I have shared with you here and become a legendary salesperson. Remember that there is no "right" way. There is only your way.

If you are Genuine, your ego and doubts will never get in your way.

If you create your Unique Sales Persona, you will never be lost in the crowd.

If you focus on building Rapport with clients, you will connect easily with them.

If you help clients get to their Unique Buying Position, you will give them a tremendous gift.

And if you become your client's Sales Ally, you will always have friends and an open door.

I can think of no greater skills to give you as you begin this "journey of a thousand miles." After all, the point of life is to enjoy the journey through it. You should enjoy every moment. That includes all the moments with your clients and every moment of your sales career.

In closing I'd like to thank you for the money you invested in this book and, even more, the time you invested in reading it. I hope it has been and will continue to be a resource for you as you go for ward in your career. I am honored to have been one of the guides on your journey.

The truth is that getting everything you dream about in life is pretty simple. You don't need complex sales strategies or to bust your hump day in and day out. It all starts with one simple choice. You must simply choose who you want to BE.

~~ Erik Luhrs
Butler, New Jersey, USA

THOUGHTS AND THANKS

What you just read hurt! Writing this book was at times painful for me. This is odd considering that I have written four screenplays and numerous short stories and started multiple novels.

Yes, there was a time in my life when you couldn't STOP Me from writing. But it has been almost a decade since those days, and my writing wings were VERY rusty when I started this book.

The other reason it hurt is because GURUS has always been a fluid thing for me. As you read the book you discovered many concepts and techniques that are part of *The GURUS Selling System*; but just like computer technology, by the time it gets to market the technology is already outdated.

GURUS never stops evolving, growing and changing because, simply, I keep working with new mentors and learning new things. I then roll what is useful into the GURUS System so folks like you can use it ASAP!

I have no secrets. I want you to know everything I can teach you as fast as I can get it to you.

So putting the "system" in a concrete form was almost heresy to me.

Nonetheless, I understand that everyone needs a foundation to start from. You can't get to black belt before being a white belt…unless you're Elvis Presley. But that is another story….

Anyway, I'd like to take this opportunity to thank the folks who made this book possible.

First, you! If you weren't reading this book then it would have no bearing on your life or sales at all, and that would be a bummer! So, thanks for reading!

Next, I'd like to thank my parents and siblings, who have always been there to show me the true meaning of the word "love"…Now if someone would teach *them* what the word means we'd be in business! Just kidding! I luv ya!

I'd like to especially thank all the mentors whose teaching and experience helped me create *The GURUS Selling System*. As is the stuff of legend now, many of those folks are unhappy that I was able to distill what they do and how they do it more effectively than they do…without giving them tons of undue monetary compensation or credit! But I still couldn't have done it without you. So, thank you!

Many thanks to my test readers: Karen Pasqualucci, Kelle Sparta, Gene Plotkin, BonnieJean Butler, Andrew Ive, Wess Schmidt, Leslie Orr and Ann Clifford. Your feedback was invaluable in making this book more useful for readers.

A huge thank you to Geoff Steck! Your trained eye, world of experience and editorial comments made this book into a real BOOK! A thousand thank-yous are not enough!

Of course, I have to thank my steadfast uber-mentor, Stephan Stavrakis, who has been there through thick and thin and just plain BLAH and always brought me back to my senses and focused me forward. You are a prince among men!

Finally, thanks to my beautiful wife, Miroslawa (Mirka), and my wonderful daughters, Charlotte and Daphne. You are the lights of my life! You are why I live and breathe! I love you and I thank you!

Oh yes, I almost forgot my dog, Dexter! You rock, little buddy! Now…get off the couch!

About the Author

ERIK LUHRS has worked with corporate America for over two decades, helping companies of all sizes, from Fortune 500 to solo-preneurs. He founded The GURUS Selling System in 2009 after 2+ years of studying with many of the top Sales and Marketing pros in the world. He continues to train with new "gurus" so that he may expand the system and make it easier and more effective for everyone. He lives with his family in New Jersey.

FOR MORE LESSONS ON HOW TO USE AND APPLY
THE GURUS SELLING SYSTEM
OR FOR MORE INFORMATION VISIT. . .

WWW.GURUSELLING.COM

Made in the USA
Lexington, KY
18 September 2012